THERAPY WITH CHILDREN

Other titles in the UKCP Series:

What is Psychotherapeutic Research?
Del Loewenthal
Diversity, Discipline and Devotion in Psychoanalytic Psychotherapy: Clinical and Training Perspectives
Gertrud Mander
Shakespeare on the Couch
Michael Jacobs
Dialogue and Desire: Mikhail Bakhtin and the Linguistic Turn in Psychotherapy
Rachel Pollard
Our Desire of Unrest: Thinking About Therapy
Michael Jacobs
Not Just Talking: Conversational Analysis, Harvey Sacks' Gift to Therapy
Jean Pain
The Muse as Therapist: A New Paradigm for Psychotherapy
Heward Wilkinson
The Emergent Self: An Existential–Gestalt Approach
Peter Philippson
Psychosis in the Family: The Journey of a Psychotherapist and Mother
Janet C. Love
Hidden Twins: What Adult Opposite Sex Twins Have To Teach Us
Olivia Lousada
Child-Centred Attachment Therapy: the Ccat Programme
Alexandra Maeja Raicar
The Three-Point Therapist
Hilary A. Davies
The Use of Psychoanalytic Concepts in Therapy with Families: For All Professionals Working with Families
Hilary Davies
Love: Bondage or Liberation: A Psychological Exploration of the Meaning, Values, and Dangers of Falling in Love
Deirdre Johnson
The Role of Brief Therapies in Attachment Disorders
Lisa Wake

THERAPY WITH CHILDREN

An Existential Perspective

Chris Scalzo

On behalf of the United Kingdom Council
for Psychotherapy

Routledge
Taylor & Francis Group
LONDON AND NEW YORK

First published 2010 by Karnac Books Ltd.

Published 2019 by Routledge
2 Park Square, Milton Park, Abingdon, Oxon OX14 4RN
52 Vanderbilt Avenue, New York, NY 10017

First issued in hardback 2019

Routledge is an imprint of the Taylor & Francis Group, an informa business

British Library Cataloguing in Publication Data

A C.I.P. for this book is available from the British Library

Edited, designed and produced by The Studio Publishing Services Ltd
www.publishingservicesuk.co.uk
e-mail: studio@publishingservicesuk.co.uk

ISBN 13: 978-0-367-10648-5 (hbk)
ISBN 13: 978-1-85575-730-1 (pbk)

CONTENTS

ACKNOWLEDGEMENTS

I would like to thank everyone whose input and support allowed me the opportunity to complete this book. I am enormously indebted to my partner, Elizabeth, for all her words of encouragement and patience throughout the process, and the richness she brings to my life each day.

Many thanks to Simon Tucker, Andy Black, and Ernesto Spinelli for their input or words of encouragement. In particular, I would also like to express my gratitude to Robert Nash for his invaluable comments and responses to early drafts. I am also very grateful to all of my colleagues at the Essex County Council, Community CAMHS team, and the South West Essex Specialist Community Children's Service. Without your feedback and support, the production of this book may not have happened.

I am fortunate enough to have been inspired and encouraged by many great therapists and educators from the "existential therapy" community, including John Heaton, Lucia Moja-Strasser, Darren Wolf, Anthony Stadlen, and Mike Harding. I wish to thank them all for their motivation and wisdom.

Words cited in conversation (Chapter Five) are reprinted with thanks, and with permission of John Heaton. My thanks also to

Faber and Faber for their permission to reprint the poetry of Sylvia Plath (Chapter Three).

Most of all I wish to express my gratitude to all of the children and young people I have been privileged enough to work with over the years. They have opened my eyes to the world and its endless possibilities.

The case examples and summaries used throughout the book are taken from my own recordings of meetings and sessions with a range of children and their families/carers in a variety of different settings. These recordings can only ever be representative of one personal and subjective perspective of each encounter. Although personal details have been changed, along with any specific information that may disclose the identity of the child involved, they have been recorded as faithfully and honestly as possible.

ABOUT THE AUTHOR

Chris Scalzo is a UKCP registered existential psychotherapist. He currently works full-time for the National Health Service as a therapist and clinical supervisor and is part of a county-wide specialist Child & Adolescent Mental Health Service (CAMHS). He has previously lectured and taught post-MA psychologists in training on Existential Psychotherapy & Counselling, and has previously published philosophically based articles in the journal *Existential Analysis*. He has worked as a therapist with children and families across a wide range of settings and in his present role provides extensive training and specialized consultation to professionals from Health, Social Care, Education, and the Voluntary sector. He is particularly interested in working with existential challenges faced by children living with physical and learning disabilities and their families, and direct work in special needs school constitutes a large part of his practice.

To Ophelia and Daniel, thank you for the love and hugs:
True relatedness in every sense.

PREFACE

Rhys

Rhys was referred by his teacher. At the time he attended a special needs school for children who had been diagnosed with moderate learning difficulties. He was twelve years old. On the referral, it said he had described himself as "attractive" on the outside and "unattractive" on the inside. He had recently passed a written note to his teacher, which said, "I can't stand life."

Rhys was normally keen to attend our sessions, often knocking on the door of the room before the appointments, asking if it was time for me to see him. In one session, he had asked if we could model faces out of clay, and he was quite insistent that I should participate. He decided his face would be "crazy". We discussed the idea of crazy, and what he thought this meant, and Rhys concluded that he, too, felt "crazy" much of the time. As he modelled, we spoke about his home and school life, and he asked many questions about my personal life, comparing his circumstances with mine. He thought he recognized me from his previous, mainstream school (although I had never actually visited this school before).

At his current school Rhys said that he has no one to play with at break time. We discussed the way in which he looked back on his previous school, viewing it as such a perfect and idealized place, and yet this was a school at which he had become extremely unpopular among staff and pupils, due to his aggressive and violent behaviour, eventually becoming excluded.

He often discussed "his ADHD", which he said his mother had known about for some time, but he could not remember the process of being diagnosed with himself. Without his medication, he said he becomes sick. On one occasion, he drew a computer screen which had ADHD written on it, and this, too, went "crazy", with electric sparks flying off from it. When it had its medication, it began to calm down, but it eventually destroyed itself. Rhys had then spoken briefly about his father for the first time. When I asked him about his feelings, however, he physically turned away.

From time to time, Rhys also discussed his passion for skateboarding with me. He explained how he would fearlessly jump from great ramps and enjoyed doing tricks; how he thought about each trick, but sometimes changed it, and how fellow skateboarders would bang their boards in applause when he successfully completed a good trick or stunt. He told me how it felt better than anything else in the world, better than football and running, both of which he excelled at.

Rhys also excelled creatively, and he regularly chose to draw in our sessions. He viewed his own work very negatively, however, and frequently told me it was all rubbish. It was common for Rhys to destroy what he had created, every few sessions either screwing up and tearing pictures, or smashing models he might have made. During one session, he chose to smash the "crazy" face he had made; in a frenzied attack, he hammered it with his fists, and then stamped on it repeatedly with the heel of his shoe until it had been broken into hundreds of tiny pieces. He told me it was all crap and I should not have saved it. As the session progressed, he became more agitated and asked to leave, although he chose not to go. He told me it would be better if the whole school burnt down. He told me that all the staff and children could die, along with the building, and that they were all "spastics". He then said that he was "spastic", too.

Throughout my work with Rhys, his moods fluctuated between extremes. Sometimes, he would act as an extremely caring, parental figure, regularly looking after and nurturing younger or more vulnerable children, shepherding them round the school. At other times, he struggled to manage his outward environment, and, as he perhaps identified more with the other children at his school, he began to detest it, rejecting them, himself, and the institution. He chose to destroy not only his work, but the building itself, often breaking up the fabric of the place, and verbally bullying less able pupils, who were unable to defend themselves. Rhys tussled with his own sense of identity. At twelve years of age he faced a huge crisis of his own existential identity. He struggled to find a firm sense of his own autonomous identity, in order that he could relate simply as one human being to another. He did not "fit in" with the rules and regulations of a normal, mainstream comprehensive school, and yet he felt out of place within the environment of "special needs" education. Rhys felt his ADHD diagnosis gave him both a lack of control and, at the same time, an identity: a way of being in the world. Through his way of being with me (in our relationship), there was an attempt to reconstruct *his* way of being himself in his world.

The temporality and challenges of life affect us all. Their proximity, however, is something autonomous, holding us close at times, and drifting away at others. During childhood, for many of us, an understanding of time and our own identity is as far from our thoughts as it will ever be, but for others, the mortality and vividness of life, which time can thrust upon us, are all too real.

What is existential psychotherapy?

Existential psychotherapy and counselling draws its frame of reference from a philosophical tradition rather than medical or diagnostic principles. Unlike other, more prescriptive approaches, existential therapy acknowledges that within all our lives we may face times when our own particular struggles can feel overwhelming. "Existential phenomenology" takes the human condition as the focus of investigation, and therapy focuses on the uniqueness of each individual's experience.

Through the therapeutic relationship, existential practice creates an opportunity for children to develop new awareness of the challenges they feel confronted with and, therefore, uncover new choices and paths in overcoming life's emotional difficulties. By building self-knowledge and self-awareness, children are able to grow and conquer issues which may, at times, feel all-consuming or overwhelming. Suffering from severe anxiety or panic attacks, for example, can be addressed through an understanding that anxiety is not similar to a virus that can be caught (in the same manner as a cold or flu), but is the outcome of choices we have made in the past, and can make in the future, in life and in the context we find ourselves in.

By exploring the context or "world view" of the child in therapy, it becomes possible to understand these choices and create new opportunities to develop and see a way out of personal suffering. In exploring our relationships, we also explore the way that everything we do is dependent on the context of our lives. The flexible and relational nature of existential psychotherapy makes it a relevant and useful approach for the hugely varied and individual challenges life presents to each one of us during childhood.

Working through an existential approach with adult clients requires the therapist to offer an attitude of openness: to be open to the client and to respect their world view, as opposed to impressing our own judgements and assumptions upon them. This is no different when working with children.

Existential psychotherapy, however, is a broad church. Although less well known in Britain, compared with the larger, more dominant theoretical approaches of psychoanalysis, cognitive behavioural therapies, family systemic, and person-centred/humanistic psychotherapy, it is a growing school comprising several differing strands (see Cooper, 2003 for further discussion of this). The main schools behind existential psychotherapy today are the American existential–humanistic, the Daseinanalysts (based primarily in Europe), and a growing British school of psychotherapy, whose main protagonists include Professors Ernesto Spinelli and Emmy van Deurzen. There are many differences between these various forms of existential psychotherapy and the ideas of their individual practitioners, often subtle, and occasionally dramatic. However, to fully explore these here would take us away from the primary task, which is to seek to demonstrate how key understandings of existential thought not only can, but indeed should, influence the practice of psychotherapy with children. Within this book, I shall acknowledge certain commonalities between the various approaches, but I will also focus on my own understanding of what is important in existential psychotherapy and how this relates to therapeutic practice with children. This probably has a closer adherence to the philosophical grounding of the modern British school of existential psychotherapy and, most importantly, to the philosophical work of Martin Heidegger.

While it is possible to see the importance of certain core constituents of existential psychotherapy, which are described and reflected upon in more detail below, it is equally important to establish what this book does not attempt to do. This book does not aim to set out a blueprint, or manual, for the practice of existential psychotherapy with children, for existential psychotherapy is fundamentally not a single system or theory for practice. I hope, however, to reflect on certain essential notions shared by philosophers and psychotherapists and, through these views, encourage an opportunity for personal reflection on the way we aim to engage children and may hope to in the future.

It is also worth adding that the demand, and possibly "need", for psychotherapy and counselling for children and young people appears to be growing, and the willingness of practitioners from a whole range of professional backgrounds and trainings to engage actively in addressing this demand is similarly great. Existentially influenced practitioners constitute an ever-increasing cohort among this expanding army of counsellors and psychotherapists working with children, and yet the development of new literature or training in this area seems to have been almost completely ignored. This book aims to redress this imbalance by considering the possibilities that arise from personal examples of employing phenomenological and existential philosophies when working psychotherapeutically with children.

Philosophical background

A brief introduction to Heidegger and psychotherapy

This book diverges from some existing models of existential psychotherapy and philosophy, concentrating primarily on a personal exploration of the phenomenology of the German philosopher, Martin Heidegger. The primary aim of this book, therefore, is to act as a reminder of the value of considering personal experiences of *psychotherapeutic* relationships, and the role these experiences play in the synthesis of dialogue. The need to reflect on our own experiences and on our individual relationship with the world is critical in understanding an existential approach to psychotherapy with children. This process of self-reflection, stimulated through dialogue, can be traced back through a history of existential philosophy, as far back as the ancient Greeks.

It is widely acknowledged that the roots of "existential" or "Continental" philosophy, as opposed to a more popular "logical" philosophy, can be traced back to the Greek sceptics. The work of Heraclitus and the questioning nature of Socratic dialogue established a way of philosophizing and enquiring into the human condition that insisted that we include ourselves as the subject. Unlike the position of much contemporary philosophy, the inclusive nature of existential thought tells us that we cannot exclude ourselves from any exploration of the real, fundamental questions of life. If, for example, we are to ask, "What does it mean to be a human being?", we must first acknowledge that we are asking this question from the position of being human. If we are to enquire into the nature of what language is, we must acknowledge that this is a question we are asking from the ironic starting position of using language ourselves. This manner of "already existing in things" is not merely accidental, and many existential thinkers, (including Heidegger), place understanding this inseparable relationship to the world as key to understanding what it is to be human.

This inclusive and ever questioning process of enquiry can be traced through the work of subsequent philosophers, such as Michel de Montaigne in the sixteenth century, and, later, in the nineteenth century literary writings of both Soren Kierkegaard and Friedrich Nietzsche. Both writers employed a highly poetic and evocative style to entice the reader to consider their philosophical positions and to implicitly communicate their own ideas, rejecting a rational position in favour of personalized and free thought, which ultimately leads to individual responsibility. As Kierkegaard wrote in his journals, "There are many people who reach their conclusions about life like schoolboys: they cheat their master by copying the answer out of a book without having worked the sum out for themselves" (Bretall, 1973, p. 19). The position Kierkegaard adopts throughout his writing is one which draws us back to the need to have considered our own position through personal thought and process. This is a central theme in the idea of existential phenomenology, and hugely relevant for its influence on the practice of psychotherapy. As we shall see later in the book, the development of an existential phenomenology gathered momentum through the twentieth century, and was influenced most conspicuously by the German philosopher, Martin Heidegger.

The name of Heidegger and the volume of work developed from his ideas and thoughts will, no doubt, be familiar to anyone with an interest in, or knowledge of, modern philosophy, but the central role he could play in influencing the practice of existential psychotherapy has only relatively recently begun to be explicitly acknowledged (See Cohn, 1997, 2002). The influence of his work on the practice of psychological therapies primarily grew from the work of two Swiss medical practitioners. The first, Ludwig Binswanger, was a psychiatrist who developed an interest in the writing of Edmund Husserl (principally his work on the development of a phenomenological methodology), and then, subsequently, the early teachings of Heidegger. The second was the psychoanalyst Medard Boss, who began a written correspondence in 1947 with Martin Heidegger and later developed a relationship that gave rise to a series of influential lectures and seminars, which became known as the "Zollikon Seminars". These discourses eventually laid the theoretical foundation for the creation of a new school of psychotherapeutic practice, later called "Daseinsanalyse". This literally translates as "there, being, analysis", or the analysis of being-there, and is a direct acknowledgement of Heidegger's understanding of what it is to be a human being in the world, "Being-in-the-world". The word *Dasein* was used by Heidegger to represent our own human existence. Essentially, it suggests that we are living beings occupying a specific space and time in the world.

Although both Binswanger and Boss developed relationships with Freud himself, Binswanger as a friend who often laboured to try to include Freud's theoretical models into his own practice, and Boss through being analysed by him as a young man, they struggled with his compulsion to define psychoanalysis as a science of intrapsychic processes. Both expressed reservations about Freud's theories and his dependence on the role of natural determinism, and from the work of Heidegger, it was possible for them to see an alternative to the subject–object, Cartesian view that so influenced the practice of psychoanalysis of their time and continues to do so today.

Thus, the foundations were laid for the practical influence of an existential phenomenology in therapeutic analysis, and, although Heidegger himself ironically refused to be called an "existentialist", the legacy of his work and dialogue continues to be the cornerstone for practice in this field. The label of "existentialist" was used by the philosopher Gabriel Marcel negatively towards Jean-Paul Sartre in the 1940s, and it appears that Sartre, liking the term, chose to adopt it, and later go on to further define it himself. Although Sartre popularized the use of the term existentialism, and it was subsequently applied to many philosophers and writers, Heidegger still chose to distance himself from it. He claimed that his primary task was to wrestle with this notion of "Being" and not with the ethics of personal existence. Heidegger's legacy, however, has clearly been not only to provoke these strong challenges to the work of subsequent philosophers and writers, such as Jean-Paul Sartre and Albert Camus, but also to strongly influence processes of psychotherapeutic practice. There are also those, in addition to Sartre, including Maurice Merleau-Ponty and R. D. Laing, who were able to develop and sometimes popularize a variety of existential themes affecting the fields of psychology, psychotherapy, and literature.

CHAPTER ONE

Questioning and assumptions

> "The real is a closely woven fabric . . . Perception is not a science of the world, it is not even an act, a deliberate taking up of a position; it is the background from which all acts stand out, and is presupposed by them"
>
> (Merleau-Ponty, 2002, p. xi)

> "Science manipulates things and gives up living in them. It makes its own limited models of things; operating upon these indices or variables to effect whatever transformations are permitted by their definition, it comes face to face with the real world only at rare intervals"
>
> (Merleau-Ponty, 1992, p. 159)

Much psychotherapy practised with children today seeks to objectify. Attempts to interpret what happens in a therapeutic relationship effectively close down possibilities and narrow the dialogue created towards a sense of "truth". Existential psychotherapy does not do this. It aims to understand, not interpret. It does not seek an objective truth, or a quality of essential truth—a truth of essence. Instead, it uses the discourse of phenomenology to create awareness, and possibility. Analysis, as Heidegger tells us (in the "Zollikon Seminars", Heidegger, 2001), is rooted in a definition of "breaking free", not restricting, and it is the child who can be offered an opportunity to break free of, or transcend, their (family) history to become an individual. This is not an easy task, and not always immediately desirable by the family and professionals alike, but it is, I believe, the responsibility of the therapist to work towards this process.

The existential psychotherapist, Hans Cohn, wrote about the need for psychotherapy to break free and create possibilities when discussing the concept of hermeneutic understanding;

> We can see that Schleiermacher's view of interpretation as "understanding" gives the concept a range of meaning considerably wider than when used by most psychotherapists. Psychodynamic interpretation is, as a rule, the discovery of the "latent" meaning behind the "manifest" content of an utterance or symptoms , whereby what "appears" is considered only a disguise for what is "real". [Cohn, 2005, p. 222]

The conventional psychodynamic therapy to which Cohn refers here has historically drawn psychotherapy towards a place alongside natural science. The predominating trend within the British National Health Service, and perhaps more widely in society, too, is for psychotherapy and, indeed, all "talking therapies" to become more quantifiable, moving towards an objectification and medicalization of psychotherapy. Natural science in itself carries out useful and helpful work. Recent developments have pushed not only modern medicine, but science in general, into new and exciting fields of neurology, and, by and large, a greater understanding of the world around us. Difficulties arise, however, when science tries to impinge on areas beyond objectification, such as what it means to be human—to be. Being is not a science.

Objectivity

Being, as Heidegger tells us, is a matter of coping with the world: being able to get around, and manage with day-to-day life. It is about how we understand the world, and we cannot step outside of our being in order to better understand it. We are simply unable, as living human beings, to step outside ourselves and observe what it means to be. In short, I cannot take leave of my consciousness in order to objectively reason what life actually is. I always have a certain perspective. Yet, through so much psychotherapy and psychological practice, people search for truths, for definitive systems, or ways to define what is "truly" happening for their client or patient. With children, this temptation seems to be even greater. Children, it seems, are categorized and objectified even further than adults. This is done by age, academic ability, medical diagnosis, behaviour, etc. Fundamentally, however, from an existential position, nothing changes. Children are still beings, actively coping with the world, trying to find their way about in the world, and with the same parameters and existential givens we must all live with.

Existential psychotherapy aims to create a discourse between child and therapist. It highlights how the existence of every one of us as living beings is defined by our choices and actions, our restrictions and our freedoms, and, at the same time, it is inescapably linked and co-defined by our relationship to the world. When a therapist arrives at a session to see and meet with a child, both parties are informed by their history and their context. The interaction is understood and interpreted by, and through, their own experiences. Certain core components of existential psychotherapy begin to emerge from this understanding of the dialogue between psychotherapist and child: *experience*, *awareness*, *choice*, and *responsibility*. When we are considering what it means to "Be", the answer is somehow revealed in our everyday existence. An answer cannot be found by thinking deep philosophical thoughts about how people came to exist, or why we are here, *but*, instead, the answer is revealed in our daily life. This notion of living, or "doing", is crucial in existential therapy. In the therapeutic context, this simply means that the therapist does not need to sit with a child or adult discussing their philosophical identity. Instead, an understanding of their world-view will be revealed through exploring their relationships with others and, in a broader sense, the world. This "dialogue" about how the child relates with others could be revealed through play, narrative, games, and so on, but, importantly, it is their creation of dialogue with the therapist that is most disclosive.

Choice

Through their very existence, children, like adults, are defined by an active, deliberate process of activity: thinking, choosing, deliberating, acting, feeling, and even writing. When writing this book, I am making a series of choices all the time. I am making choices in an immediate sense every moment I live, and I am also making choices that provide the parameters and boundaries for the overall context in which the momentary decisions I face present themselves. For example, I have chosen to sit in my office and not play with my children or watch television: this is not, in itself, a decision about what I will be writing, but it creates a context for writing. Both context and choice are paramount for existential psychotherapy with children. Within existential thought, the importance of making (indeed, having to make) choices in our life is twofold. The first important aspect we must recognize is in defining who we are. To be human is not to be a defined, individual self, with a mysterious inner world and set characteristics. Instead, we are always an action, a choice if you will, relating to the world in which we live. The second notion, to which it is important to attend, is the experience of guilt that may arise from the choices we make. While we are always making certain choices in our daily lives, even if these are not acknowledged, there are always, by definition, options and choices that are not chosen. This guilt is, therefore, not the same sensation as feeling guilty about something (for example, I could have tried harder in that exam), but it is, instead, an existential guilt; rather, it defines our existence. Through psychotherapy, it is possible to understand our inherent inability in life to obtain completeness and acknowledge our inevitable shortcomings by not realizing every possibility we face. For children, this can come through exploration of the possibilities they face but often fail to reflect upon.

For change to occur through therapeutic exploration, there must still exist a motivation to make it happen. When working with a child, it is possible to encourage reflection and awareness of their circumstances, and, hence, the choices they are making. Subsequently, it is also possible to offer options, different ways of being, therefore presenting them with choices. The timid, withdrawn child, who struggles to socialize with his peers, may be able to develop enough trust in the therapeutic space or relationship to become more playful and less boundaried. In turn, this relaxation of guarded and defensive behaviour allows them to develop new experiences and confront possible fearful alternatives. Perhaps the greatest challenge, however, is not in grasping these optional choices wholeheartedly, but of encouraging the realization that choices exist. When, often, destructive behaviours appear as "compulsive" habits, they are simply reactionary choices upon which there has been little or no reflection. We could say they are pre-reflective behaviours. These may include aggressive behaviour, over-eating, excessive drinking or drug taking, and many more. It is also important to emphasize, however, that these behaviours could still be the repercussions of reflective choices (depending on circumstances). In order to address this behaviour, it is vital to focus on the here-and-now quality of the relationship in therapy with a child. This exploration presents experiences illustrative of the child's experiences of the world, and will allow them to focus on reassuming responsibility, for, once they are responsible for what has gone wrong, then they can also assume responsibility for rectifying it (Yalom, 2008).

Choosing psychotherapy

The first step of any journey is making the decision to take the trip. In therapy, this decision comes, for client and therapist, right at the start of their journey together. Prior to the first session, there is a point at which a client decides to make a disruption to their world: a decision to change or shake up what has become familiar or accepted. To begin a therapeutic journey, a decision has to be made by the client to put themselves in a position for something new to happen. In basic terms, when something has become stuck or difficult to manage, whether this is brought to the fore by someone they know or someone they have never met, there is still always a decision for that person either to engage in a therapeutic process, their journey, or to choose not to. Even when the client is compelled to sit in front of a therapist by a person in authority, there is ultimately a choice as to how that person chooses to engage. Whether people are referred to me by their doctor, or whether their partner metaphorically drags them to a session, how they choose to engage with me is their choice, and, ultimately, theirs alone. They can really choose to explore their understanding of the world, to engage fully in a new relationship, or they may choose simply to attend.

For children, the choice to attend therapy is rarely their own. Even when a child may express a desire to attend sessions to see someone they understand to be a counsellor or psychotherapist, or the man who makes you "well in the head", unless they are deemed mature enough to make an informed choice about their subsequent "treatment", a responsible adult must consent on their behalf. How, then, can working with children ever be truly therapeutic? How can children ever take the first step on that journey themselves? Each time a child attends a session on a particular day, they are confronted with a choice: how much of their emotional world and experiences will they choose to reveal or expose, and how much will they buy in to this new and novel relationship? Regardless of age, these choices are always present.

What is this therapeutic relationship? How do we know if it is something to which both therapist and child are committed? What brings a child to a therapeutic relationship, and how can this be understood?

Daniel

Daniel was seven years old when first referred to me by a community paediatrician. He was wetting the bed and suffered what were described as "night terrors" by his parents. His behaviour at school was becoming hard for his teachers to manage; he was frequently violent towards his peers, and he had been excluded from school on several occasions. When I met his parents for the first time, Daniel had been asked to attend school only during the morning, and his parents felt that his actions were placing unmanageable levels of stress on all the family relationships. During this first meeting with Daniel's parents, they described how his behaviour had always been difficult, and his father added that he would never have been able to behave as Daniel did during his own childhood.

As they continued to describe their situation, they began to reveal certain inconsistencies in their approach to parenting: his father was very authoritative and emotionally "cut off" from his son, saying quite candidly that he found it hard to love him; and, as if to compensate for this, his mother was overwhelmingly affectionate towards him, and, through her guilt, found it hard to put in any appropriate boundaries or discipline. The more he misbehaved, the harder it became for his father to feel close to him, and their relationship was on an accelerating downward spiral.

Daniel also had a younger sister, four years of age, who appeared to be favoured in differing ways by both parents, although particularly by Daniel's father. It was clearly noticeable that Daniel had been the less favoured child in the family for much of his life. The father would spend much more time playing with Daniel's sister, and was always affectionate and tactile towards her, allowing her to sit upon his lap and cuddle up to him whenever she chose. At home, she shared the parent's bedroom, while Daniel slept separately, in his own room. When I first saw Daniel and his father together, they shared absolutely no physical contact throughout the entire fifty-minute session, despite being given many opportunities to display affection.

At home, Daniel had begun to enact more and more resentment towards his sister, and had started to refuse to use the same cutlery and crockery as her to eat from. He still wanted to play with her, but had become outwardly possessive of his own toys and did not want her to touch them.

After agreeing to work with Daniel, I started seeing him alone for weekly sessions, but it soon became clear his father's presence would also be beneficial. When I collected Daniel from the waiting area, he was always keen and enthusiastic about attending, and frequently ran the short distance to the room for our session. It was noticeable, however, that when his father also attended, he would still run to the room, but then stop before entering, choosing instead to hide under a table. Initially, I asked if he wished for me to invite him into the room, but he was quite clear that he wanted his father to do this. He said he would come straight into the room if his father invited him in, and, true to his word, when his father asked him to come in, he did. Each week, this scenario became an established ritual, and each week, his father would have to make the same request, for him to come into the room.

When we reflected on this situation, Daniel's father said that he felt highly embarrassed by Daniel's behaviour, clearly expecting me to be disappointed in some way by his actions. For his part, Daniel showed his appreciation of his father by increasingly encouraging him into his play. At first, Daniel chose not to speak to his father directly, but instead he acted out any responses to his questions through a silent mime. This, again, was a regular occurrence in each session, but later became increasingly playful. It was not long before both Daniel and his father smiled and laughed at each mime performed. Despite the challenges they both felt in allowing themselves to engage in a new and different way, it was not long before Daniel's father was an integral part of all of their narrative and creative play.

The choices Daniel made in attending and engaging were vitally important to how he used the time. It seemed that he was very pleased to have the opportunity to come to our sessions himself, but that his father's attendance (despite being something we had explored together) set a different context for his decision making. Their past and outside experiences together where somehow very present. The significance of wanting to be invited into the room by his father was revealing of their relationship beyond our sessions. I felt strongly that Daniel had a desire to be "invited into the family" in some way, and the opportunity to express that was valuable. This brief example illustrates how the choice to attend therapeutic sessions is present for even very young children, and shows how the challenges in truly deciding to engage in a relationship are equally strong for both adults and children. It was not necessary to look for a hidden meaning behind Daniel's actions and behaviours. The opportunity was simply created for the disclosure of possibilities in the relationship to be revealed. It was important to view Daniel's relationship with his father as setting part of the context for their possibilities, and, at the same time, to be circumspect as to how these choices became evident. Daniel created choices both for himself, through his own awareness, and for his father. If my focus was purely on interpretation of their actions, it would be drawing me away from what was being shown.

CHAPTER TWO

A theory of existential practice with children

> "Theoretical behaviour is just looking, without circumspection"
>
> (Heidegger, 2000, p. 99)

Before considering how a theory of existential psychotherapy with children would look, it is first necessary to consider how appropriate it would be to develop an all-encompassing theory of "existential child psychotherapy".

Circumspection means to look around. This seems to be completely opposed to theory, which looks in one direction. In examining theory, the reader is looking for something, categorizing it, and jumping ahead of the text they are actually reading. A theory is formulated and examined in much the same way as a calculation. A calculation employs a process, which is already determined in some manner, since it must obey a pre-existing set of mathematical rules. We cannot, for example, decide to multiply in a new and original way. If a psychotherapist or counsellor aims to be truly open to the presentation of a child, then a theory must not be at the forefront of the engagement. If the therapist engages "theoretically" in a session with a child, it encourages him or her to be aware of what might be coming, and, in doing so, make what is close at hand further away; it confers to them an expectation or an idea of what is intended, but may not be realized. When travelling to work in the morning for my first session of the day, I might often be ahead of myself, in some way. In other words, I am perhaps thinking about how the child may arrive, whether they will be on time, how the session may go, and so on. What I am actually least attentive to is what I am actually doing: driving. This has become a pre-reflective activity. Similarly, within a session with a child, if I am too focused on how they may present themselves, and how their behaviour should be categorized or interpreted, what I am least attentive to is what is actively being revealed in our relationship.

Anticipation inevitably acts as a lens through which the child is encountered and understood, colouring the therapist's perspective. Something that is observed through a lens is seen in a certain way. Lenses have the ability to both enhance and distort, depending on the viewer's perspective, but the original perceptions of the viewer are always changed. This is a danger, since the primary experiences and understanding of each session and therapeutic encounter with a child are paramount.

Despite these dangers, it would be somewhat naïve, however, to suggest that it is possible for a psychotherapist to arrive at a session with no prior information or knowledge of the child they are about to see, nor, in many contexts, would it be appropriate. As discussed previously, children and young people are almost always referred to a therapist by an interested third party and not by themselves: school, parent, social worker, and doctor, etc. Each referral inevitably brings with it a trail of information. Indeed, as Spinelli highlights (2007), the manner by which a client arrives at a session, both literally and metaphorically, is rarely considered at length by many therapists, but contains information and wisdom of understanding a client that can be incredibly revealing. This is never truer than with children and young people. It is important for the practitioner to consider the understanding and expectations of people making referrals and this can often reveal huge conflicts in the experiences and world-view of a child, highlighting things that may not otherwise be clearly presented. By the very referral itself, someone else has noticed or observed a behaviour or presentation in a child that concerned them sufficiently, and they subsequently wished for it to be explored or "disturbed". A child identified as behaving badly in school, for example, may ultimately be referred to a counsellor or psychotherapist, but the teacher who struggles with managing their "bad" behaviour is normally not.

Thus, this book aims not to comprehensively answer or address all of the dilemmas and factors salient to working with children, but hopes to encourage processes of reflection and questioning, consequently informing the practice of anyone who does.

Categorization and diagnosis

It should not be the aim of the psychotherapist to diagnose a child, although families, schools, medical professionals, and officers of the court frequently request this. Any form of existential psychotherapy should be inherently against the *fixed* and *deterministic* categorization that diagnosis brings. Intrinsic within providing diagnoses is the belief, or world-view, that our behaviours or difficulties can be pathologized. An existential approach to psychotherapy recognizes and considers the various experiences life can bring. This involves the understanding that, from time to time, life can be difficult and challenging, and it is the role of the therapist to consider and help to clarify these issues.

When working with children in any context, however, there exists the temptation to categorize them. This can be done according to their age, understanding, or cognitive abilities, a "medical" model of diagnosis (e.g., ADHD), emotional literacy, styles of "attachment", and so on. Even the definition of a person as a "child" involves a level of categorization that is easily overlooked or given little attention by some professionals. Clearly, there are legal and ethical guidelines for this definition, which vary between one culture and another, but these are informed by the values of each society. There are many examples of this, such as the age at which it is deemed acceptable to marry, join the military, buy alcohol or tobacco, and consent to medical treatment or psychotherapy. It seems difficult to suggest which of these criteria should inform the judgement of categorizing someone as a child (and this is, perhaps, a separate debate); however, an awareness of the subjective judgements we make is integral when trying to understand a child and engage them in therapeutic discourse.

The importance of recognizing these judgements and assumptions is not with a view to "bracketing" them or unrealistically putting them aside, but of acknowledging them as real components of each therapeutic engagement.

When meeting with a child, there is no possibility for us to be neutral or impartial observers. Our relatedness to the world is a characteristic of human existence, and we can never subsequently be a blank screen on to which children project themselves: we are mutually engaged in inevitable *intersubjectivity*. My self-awareness and self-affirmation derive from my knowledge and awareness of the existence of others. I cannot begin with an understanding of myself as a given, and then subsequently presume the existence of other people in the same "model" as my own image or understanding. Social relations always exist, and although I can choose to try to free myself from the influence of this person or that, I am never independent from my history of living in the world or the others with which I share it.

Further therapeutic application

> The client's presentation of pathology is always to be understood as a revelation which is significant and unique. The client's presentation of pathology should appear striking and radical, it should surprise us; if it does not, then the physician or therapist has not heard the way in which this client uniquely lives out his or her illness. [Wolf, 2002, p. 302]

Here, Wolf challenges us as psychotherapists to be not only attentive to the uniqueness of each new client and each time we meet with them, but also, perhaps more controversially, to our own experience of meeting with a client. For it seems that without taking into account personal experiences, the therapist could not be aware of their surprise, and certainly not in a "striking and radical" way. This acts as a reminder to us: a relationship that is to include dialogue is not uniquely about the therapist following the child and allowing them to be, but a process of interaction and disturbance.

The benefit of a child engaging with therapy, therefore, is not in escaping or taking refuge from the world, but in confronting it.

The therapist must remember that the child they are working with can also never be understood in isolation. Although the temptation exists to see both therapist and child as separate entities joined in a common task, they are not. The other's existence is an existential given which is constitutive of being alive. The child entering into a therapeutic relationship is inescapably part of an *a priori* group or a dialogue; not necessarily an intense, in-depth conversation, but a being-with. We must identify both therapist and child as inclusive parts of the therapy they are engaged in. Thus, to place any validity on the understanding or "reality" that may arise, the therapist must reflect upon two key aspects of the relationship. First, the context in which the therapeutic process took place; second, and just as importantly, the way in which they and their interventions are included in the process.

The process of therapy, thus, becomes much like the study of history. In short, it reveals two different tiers of interpretation. In the study of history, these "two understandings" are about the period that is analysed and the period from which it is viewed. Britain's colonial history, for example, is viewed in a very different way now to how it would have been shortly after the turn of the previous century. In therapy, there exists both the presented detail of the child (their narrative) and the context from which it is understood. In a broader sense, therapy can also be revealing of our context in history, for many specific presentations of children appear to be particular to their place in time: for example, the nineteenth century prevalence of hysteria.

Innocent

Innocent, at age seven, was referred by the Special Needs Co-ordinator (SENCo) at his school for individual therapy, largely at his teacher's request. He had only been at the school for half a term, and his behaviour had already become difficult to manage and contain in the classroom. I was initially given little information about him, but had agreed regardless of this to meet with him for sessions at school. I was informed by the SENCo that Innocent and his family were recent refugee migrants from West Africa, and that this was his first experience of school in this country. He had received little or no formal education in the country of his birth. Despite this, however, his grasp of English was said to be good, and his mother was keen for him to attend both school and, later, our therapy sessions.

When I first arrived at school to see Innocent, it was clear that within this small and generally quite nurturing environment he had developed a reputation very quickly. The school secretary was aware of the purpose of my visit, and let out a large sigh as I walked past the office. "Here to see Innocent? Good luck."

Prior to our first session I met with the SENCo, who was keen to warn me of his difficult behaviour. Her anxiety was clear to see, and she was almost apologetic for making the referral, and that I had agreed to start work with him. "He probably won't stay in the room, he often runs into the playground . . . and he can often bite, as well as kick . . . and there really doesn't seem to be any pattern or trigger to his outbursts . . . if he runs out . . . if he hits you . . . well, I'll be around, you just let me know."

As I collected him from class he was running around the back of the room, smiling, and, although not engaged in the lesson, he did not appear to be distressed. He was told of my arrival and then escorted from the classroom, with both the SENCo and class teacher grasping firmly on to his hands. Once out of the class and left effectively in my care, he immediately ran off to the school hall and circled its perimeter at top speed. As I watched him, I began to worry, and fear that I may lose him before he even made it to the therapy room. Instead, I reminded myself that he did not presently seem to be a child who was distressed by his own behaviour. I winked at him, beckoned him with a turn of my head, and he soon began to follow me off to the therapy room, walking just a few feet behind. Once in the room, Innocent circled it several times, before sitting down on the floor and removing his socks and shoes. He quickly gestured for me to do the same, and although I agreed to remove my shoes, as the floor was so hard and cold I negotiated with him that I would keep my socks on. The nature of this interaction seemed to set the tone for many of our subsequent sessions. He was always happy to attend, but often liked to run to another point in the school first. He engaged in many different creative activities over the next few weeks, but we almost always seemed to become absorbed in a negotiation for every activity. Noticeably, he always wanted me to be involved in all of these activities.

Around two months into our sessions, a blanket of snow had fallen outside the therapy room. Innocent explained how he had never seen snow before coming to this country, and, as yet, he had been kept from playing in it, as he had been made to stay inside over break-time. This was apparently due to his disruptive behaviour in class. As our session began, he seemed to be extremely agitated, pacing quickly up and down, sighing heavily, and jumping quickly from one topic to another. He explained how he wanted to come to the session, but was overwhelmed by the thought of playing in the snow, and was unable to contain his excitement. We negotiated how he could go outside if he wished, but that the time for the sessions would have to be fixed, as I had another child to see soon after. Innocent drew a picture of a clock and marked on it the time (as he understood it) that he wanted to have. He drew a normal clock face, but increased by tenfold the number of minutes between the hours of our session. He then picked up the clock hanging on the wall and changed the time, turning the hands back. We soon did go outside, and, over the coming months, Innocent's behaviour in class did apparently become more manageable. He would sit on the carpet when asked to, he became more engaged in his lessons, and eventually stopped biting other children.

Despite the high levels of anxiety of all the school staff working with Innocent, he was always keen to attend the sessions. At the start of our first session, the worry that he could not be contained was evident from almost the whole school, and from the moment I arrived to the moment our session started, I felt inevitably caught up in this wave of apprehension. Interestingly, however, Innocent was clearly a boy who was confident in making choices and decisions. He commenced our work together with the skills to negotiate and compromise and only really became greatly distressed when his expectations to do so were strongly challenged. Through the difficulties and dilemmas he discussed with me, it emerged that, in many ways, he had begun to educate the people around him through his ability to compromise. He felt able to exercise some control when provided with a safe environment, and he offered the same opportunities to his teacher. The amount of new experiences for him, and the inevitable anxiety these were sometimes going to bring, could not be taken away through therapy, but the ability to negotiate the systems around them, and find a pathway he was comfortable with, could be developed. This was illustrated through his attempt to manipulate time; although I chose not to broaden the limits of our session, he was able to exercise some of his own control and facilitate his own feelings of safety and security.

My expectation before working with Innocent was that he would be wild and uncontained. This is the message I was given, and, on reflection, it was perhaps inevitable that I, too, would feel anxious with him. Innocent seemed to live with anxiety and uncertainty, and these were almost familiar to him. He created these emotions, and, in some ways, these emotional responses left him in control. I did not consider it my role to ignore and put aside my own anxieties and worries, but instead to reflect on how these feelings informed my understanding of Innocent's experience of school.

Within our sessions, I hoped to offer an alternative context in which to choose and develop alternative ways of feeling safe and comfortable at school.

It is impossible for any therapist to merely remain a casual observer in a therapeutic relationship, in the same way that it is impossible for us to contemplate life without some acknowledgement that we are ourselves living beings, as Heidegger says, "Being-in-the-world". The most dangerous and potentially obtrusive assumptions during therapy are those that we do not perceive ourselves to have made. The danger exists here because these judgements are, by their very nature, not reflected upon or acknowledged. When working with children, the temptation to not reflect on our language, choices and judgements is magnified. This is again echoed by the fact that children very rarely make a decision to come to see a psychotherapist themselves and, as described previously, the subsequent relationship is almost always informed by the opinion of a third party. This will inevitably influence the judgements of the psychotherapist, but should not be ignored or put aside, as these judgements inescapably illustrate an aspect of the Being of that particular child.

CHAPTER THREE

The process of child therapy

"Does the man who knows know something or nothing?"
(Socrates, from Plato, 1974)

It feels appropriate for a book that aims, in part, to initiate debate about existential considerations of therapy with children, to offer further questions and an opportunity to reflect on individual practice. This book is not a *manual* for the practice of existential psychotherapy with children. Instead, this book endeavours to function as a guide to a new land, offering individual opinions and reflections, reviews and experiences. As with a travel guide that recommends a new restaurant or hotel, the idea is that readers will be encouraged to sample this approach for themselves, develop opinions, and challenge the ideas proffered. This chapter addresses some of the key matters which must be considered when working therapeutically with children, and to reflect upon how an existential perspective on these issues may complement or question existing ways of working. In setting out practical steps for the context and introduction to therapeutic engagement, the practising therapist must remember that each new meeting or encounter with a family, professional, or child is a unique and singular experience.

In meeting a child at a particular time, in a particular way, with a certain therapist, something new has been created which cannot be transposed and objectified into a seminal moment of the process. Each encounter is unique and special, and reveals something of the child *in that moment*. Upon meeting them again in a different time or place, this is, to all intents and purposes, not the same child. We are all *active* beings in the world, projecting ourselves forward into existence. The child who attends therapy is always active, always doing, always choosing, and, as such, is not a static entity that we can assess, measure, and treat.

Again, it is important to hold in mind that each step along the path of therapeutic process should not be adopted as a component of a standard template for practice, but considered and reflected on as an individual means of engaging with children. The steps explored in the process below are aspects that have come to be essential in my practice, principally in the National Health Service and public sector, but hold relevance for both private practice and for those working with charities or voluntary organizations. Some children referred for therapy may travel neatly through the sequence of steps, in the conventional order described here, and some may not. Some steps may happen concurrently with others, and some may be repeated and revisited throughout the therapeutic journey. In the same way that each child and each encounter is different and unique, the opinion of each experienced practitioner will differ. In essence, each part of the process is simply a step towards building a therapeutic relationship, and each relationship is different. While therapists working with children may arrive with many differing approaches, and they may agree or disagree with the process outlined, it is important that they consider it their own personal responsibility to reflect on each step along the way and not assume someone else has "done the thinking" for them. When working therapeutically with children, each choice has an ethical component to its outcome, and each one may deliver great and lasting consequences in the life of a child.

Referral information

It is commonly thought in psychotherapy practised with children that the initial aim should be to gather as much information as possible. Certainly, within therapeutic practice in the public sector, there is a frequently held belief that the more relevant information that can be included within a referral, the more effective the process will be.

Most referrals for children have their origins either in an educational setting or are directly from parents themselves. When a child is referred by a doctor or social worker, it is most often because they have been contacted as an initial springboard to receiving help and support. The variety of sources is important to consider when thinking about the nature of the information delivered in referral. Just as relevant, too, is the language used to request a service.

The concerns of teachers and parents are wide and varied, and may arrive with genuine worry for a child, both well advised and misplaced. A referral may also come, however, out of the referrers' own frustration and inability actively to cope with a child. Right from the start of the therapeutic process, the existential practitioner must reflect on the language and assumptions with which they are presented. Every aspect holds with it information which begins a narrative of the changing world of the child. The way a referral arrives at the door of the therapist may be disclosive of something, the way the concerns or demands for a child are expressed may be disclosive, and the way in which the referrals are read will reveal some aspect of a potential encounter or relationship. What becomes immediately significant from an existential perspective is not so much the content itself, but the process. The style of delivery is as significant, if not more so, than the material itself.

Each step along the way should be addressed as poetry. From traditional social or medical models of child psychotherapy, it is the detail of the content that helps to build a picture of who and how a child objectively is: it was this operation which made them like this; it was this tragic loss which has made them like that; and so on. Existentially speaking, each relationship and each encounter is unique. Each experience is new, and the therapist must be open to this. It is necessary to look beyond simple explanations of cause and effect. When reading prose, we are often consumed with the narrative as the author describes an experience or situation through established patterns of spoken or written structure. Essentially, the reader assumes he shares the same understanding of the words on the page as the author who selected them. There is an assumption of shared meaning. With poetry, the reader must arrive in a more open frame of mind. When reading poetry we must expect surprise. Each word may be used in a new context, with a new emphasis or new meaning.

> Mud-mattressed under the sign of the hag
> In a clench of blood, the sleep-talking virgin . . .
>
> . . . But at the price of a pin-stitched skin
> Fish-tailed girls purchase each white leg.
>
> [Plath, 1989, p. 51]

When deciphering the poetry of Sylvia Plath, for example, the reader is instantly involved in the dialogue as it creates a challenge to be understood in a way that may also be unique to us. This poetry, like any other, can be analysed or deconstructed in a thorough exegesis, but knowing more about the details of where or how it was written do not reveal its passion or meaning; these are found through a personal engagement with the poem. Similarly, the qualities of a fine wine can be read about and discussed, but it is only in the tasting that we are able to experience what the wine *is* and enjoy it in a unique and personal way.

It is important to consider what is being requested of the therapist and how this fits into their own working paradigm. As soon as the referral has been received, work has effectively begun, as the therapist is thrust into a place of ethical judgement. The social context in which both therapist and child may find themselves may not be of their own making, or may be largely beyond their control, but it must be acknowledged and addressed in the process. When a child is referred to a therapist by a teacher, doctor, social worker, or parent, it is not a change in themselves they are requesting, but in the other. Inherent in this process is an objectification that it is the child, uniquely and singularly, who can be identified as needing to change. It is they who can be supported or "fixed". Seldom is a request from a child for a teacher to receive therapy given much consideration.

Assessment

Making an assessment involves a process of judgement. In assessing a financial investment, a business analyst might, for example, seek to assess the potential gain against the stake that must be initially invested. They might assess levels of risk by examining the history of previous performance, and then subsequently evaluate their best options for opting into this new opportunity. Alongside this leap, having made their assessment, they will no doubt have formulated a plan based on their own experiences and interpretations of the historical information gathered, in order to maximize their potential return. In short, they look at what has happened before and plan for the future. A therapeutic assessment is traditionally a process that also relies on analysis of the past in order to plan for the future: in essence, models of cause and effect.

Common to all types of assessment is a reliance on history. The therapist will need to take a thorough history of the child's symptoms or problematic behaviour, their emotional and physical development, their family history, and so on. Working through a typical model of assessment, a child may often then be assessed for their suitability to attend therapy. This could be based upon the stability of their family life or foster placement; it could be judged through their ability to engage in symbolic play or metaphor; it could be assessed through levels of self-awareness or emotional literacy. Subsequently, the most appropriate strategy will be sought to support the needs of the child, based on this assessment of the information provided.

In each relationship and in each new context, however, the child is different from before. As living beings in the world, each child is constantly making choices and relating to their environment in order to cope with the world of which they are a part. As such, they are constantly active, and, indeed, from an existential perspective, we could say they are defined by their actions and choices. At each point they are "ahead of themselves", directed towards the world, and, as such, they are changing. This view can, perhaps, be best understood by considering the process of Being as an active one, and not something that passively happens to any one of us.

There is, therefore, no set history, as such, which could be analysed in order to better understand a complete and definitive view of an individual child. In effect, the history of an individual child is only ever really disclosed in their understanding, the language they use, and the way they cope in the world, not by factual details of past events. The child's history is always in the present and something that is recounted in a specific context by a specific person. When a parent talks to their child's therapist about the history of adversity they may have faced, this will only ever be from their own perspective. A child's history is always subjective, and discloses as much about the person telling it as it does about the events themselves. When, for example, several witnesses to a crime are asked by the police to recall events describing a specific scene or incident, they rarely do so in the same way. Each account is truthful, and yet, sometimes radically contrasting.

Frequently, in assessments, a part of the child is identified and abstracted in order that it can be treated. The child may be viewed as having a certain attachment disorder, presenting a false self, being caught in a primitive developmental stage, possessing a specific and identifiable level of pathology in their internal world, and so on. Within such a pseudo-scientific paradigm, these means of assessing have the outcome of enabling a child to be identified within a preordained category for which treatment can be prescribed. Once a satisfactory assessment of the presenting symptoms is completed, many aspects of the work can be determined or mapped out. This includes decisions about which materials to use in the play or creation of narrative, how often the sessions should occur, and sometimes, as in the case of building secure attachments, which family members should also be included in the work.

This traditional perspective of assessment acts to objectify a child. If a certain technique or interpretation is to be matched to a certain presentation, then it must have something objective against which a comparison can be made. A bacterial infection must be identified in order to treat it with the appropriate antibiotic. Similarly, the particular attachment style must be identified in order that it can be addressed through the appropriate therapeutic intervention. The psychotherapist leaves the assessment with a fixed notion of how the child can be viewed. From adopting a position in which the therapist seeks to identify and make judgements about a child, they are also thrust into a position of power, and an unequal dynamic is unavoidable.

By contrast, from an existential position, the child is always evolving or "becoming" and cannot be understood through a single interpretation. The judgements a therapist will inevitably make about a child may be revealing and disclosive of their world-view, but this always includes the therapist. From an existential perspective, there is, then, no benefit to be drawn from a "therapeutic assessment" as such. To do so would simply be suggesting that the child could be objectified in a certain way, irrespective of time, place, and observer. Needless to say, such an assessment also does not take into account the influence and beliefs of the therapist themselves.

Pre-assessment

When working with children and families, however, there is also an ethical component that must be considered at every step in the process. For this reason, an assessment of the context has become an essential part of my own practice. This is not aimed at establishing a therapeutic plan or a means for establishing a relationship. Instead, this "pre-assessment" is a means for considering what has brought this child to therapy. Without considering this question, there is potential for the therapist to inadvertently act to reinforce a potentially negative situation. The child deemed to be the root of a family's instability could have this message implicitly communicated to them by "needing" to see a therapist. Alternatively, a class teacher could further understand a child's difficult behaviour as the result of "mental health" issues that require him to attend psychotherapy. In neither of these examples are the adults encouraged to look at their own part in the relationship. How do they relate to each child, and what might *they* be doing to bring about certain behaviour? If existential therapy is a process that encourages those involved to reflect on their own responsibility, this should happen for referrer and parent, as well as child and therapist. The existential approach, then, traditionally discourages any form of assessment. However, when it is applied to therapeutic work with children, this may be the only exception, as long as this is not considered a therapeutic assessment of their "internal world", but an informed context from which to consider key ethical questions.

Contracting with parents/carers

It is commonplace for therapists working with children to invite all members of the immediate family to an initial screening appointment or first assessment. This systemic approach is normally employed to enable the therapist to observe the interactions and dynamics within the family as a unit. An existentially based psychotherapy must, however, be directed more towards the possibility of the child being able to transcend their family circumstances. The family is not the client, and while relationships are indeed paramount in the context of understanding a child's worldview, the intention is not to correct a distorted way of relating. The family is not seen as an organism in itself, and, therefore, the existential concerns of the child coming to therapy should be the focus. Therapeutic work with more than one family member alongside a child should not be ruled out, but this also raises deeper questions about the aim and focus of the work.

It is important to consider the goals of meeting with parents at the onset of the therapeutic process. These will include the need to gain consent, to provide reassurance to anxious parents or, potentially, disturbance to their views of the child, and to consider not only the impact of change within a family, but also the desire for it to take place. Frequently, it is at this stage of the process in which the most disturbing and shocking behaviours within a family are exposed. As with any professional working closely with children of any age, their welfare and safety must always remain a priority. If any concerns for the safety of a child's physical or emotional well-being are to be passed on to appropriate authorities, it is preferable to be in a position to do so before therapeutic work has begun. Once a child has begun regularly to attend sessions and establish a trusting and valuable relationship, this inevitably will be altered when the therapist must share information with someone outside.

It is again important to consider here the need for space to reflect on the ethical elements of the process. The therapeutic process for children is intertwined with issues of power throughout, and it is important that many of these are recognized, both explicitly and implicitly. Many aspects of the therapeutic relationship can be considered with parents, even before the child has been met. Particularly when working in private practice or community settings, in which the therapist may be the first person to closely examine a child's circumstances, it is best initially to provide as little disruption and change to their routine as possible. It would not be appropriate for the therapist to introduce themselves and the prospect of regular therapy sessions to a young child whom they subsequently did not end up working with. During initial discussion with parents, it may emerge that the needs of the child could best be met through other means. A child about to be evicted with their family and become homeless will, of course, need first of all to be re-housed, rather than given the opportunity to build emotional resilience or explore how this situation will affect them. It may also be important for the therapist to explore with parents their expectations of the work. Do they hope the therapy will change their child? If so, in what way? This may be a suitable time to suggest that actually it might be a parent who is struggling to cope emotionally, or who may need to re-evaluate their own understanding and possibilities in therapy. This is also a process that could happen alongside work carried out with a child, but by a different therapist.

Meeting with parents and carers also presents an opportunity to remind those involved of the importance of choice. Just as it should be the parent's choice to decide if they wish to attend their own therapy, they can be reminded that the therapeutic relationship offered to their child is also a voluntary one. Often, it may be difficult for parents to reject a so-called "offer" for their child to receive counselling or therapy from an authority figure. When their child's head teacher or family doctor tells them their child *needs* to see a therapist, parents are expected to agree without questioning what this may mean. Accompanying the positive possibilities of the therapeutic work may be negative implications, or simply a feeling that the offer is not, in fact, optional, and one they may not be able to reject. Even within the care plan of a child for whom the state holds responsibility, psychotherapy may often be recommended without due consideration as to how this may impact on a child, both positively and negatively.

Therapy is often considered as a treatment, in much the same way as medication. As such, it validates the existence of an "illness" or malfunction. A doctor would not, for example, prescribe an antifungal drug without first verifying the presence of a fungal infection. The use of one is an indication of the presence of the other. In a different context, the prescribing of antidepressants could be taken as verifiable proof of the existence of a disorder or illness called depression. As a treatment, it is then also true that psychotherapy may be considered as evidence for the existence of mental illness within a child. Some notion of choice should, therefore, always be made apparent to the parents, who can also be encouraged to reflect upon how the child themselves may view this new possibility.

Parents and carers need to consider their own needs and role in the process, and to do so openly and frankly without the possibility of emotionally harming their child.

> Parents are eager and hungry to know. But, for too long they have been made to feel unable to handle what they deserve to know. Parents are puzzled . . . They worry whether they are good enough parents, whether they love enough? They doubt themselves in this way when they feel the outcroppings of animosity toward their children that most parents feel at all times. [Baruch, 1966, p. 30]

The possibility for parents to feel judged, not only by their children, but also by the therapist, is great. When they first arrive at an initial meeting with the man or woman who may potentially be their child's therapist, their anxiety may be very high, even when this was a process they instigated. The parents themselves may be in deep crisis, or have negative experiences of therapy in their own history, all of which will inevitably have an impact on their understanding of the process. In order for the therapist to set the context for an open and honest dialogue, it might be necessary for them to carefully manage their relationship and dialogue with the child's parents. The practitioner should not become a therapist for the parents, but must also lay the foundations for the future development of a process to which parents are supportive and committed. Parental anxiety may be very high, and needs to be considered gently and reassuringly. It is important for the therapist to bear in mind that the child they see for just fifty minutes a week will return to their family or carers until next week. It is possible for parents to feel "pushed out", or potentially jealous of the new and special relationship their child may be forming with the therapist. It is also possible that the parent who is obliged to manage so many aspects of a child's complete life may feel inadequate, since they are unable to provide the space to truly hear their child's pain or worries. When meeting with parents, all of these possibilities should be considered, for the potential for these relationships to have a negative impact on the child are great. Frequently, without reflection, an inadequate feeling parent may express their frustrations towards the present child, rather than the therapist, who may be unobtainable until the next session. To minimize the potential impact of these sensations, the parents may benefit from reassuring words and as thorough an understanding of the process as possible.

As with referring professionals, the parents must also understand and accept the limitations of their involvement in the work. The detail of the sessions must remain completely confidential (in the absence of any information that may put a child at risk), and any reviews or evaluations will only be to provide an opportunity for them to be reassured and discuss concerns, information, or feelings they may have. This can, of course, be a useful opportunity, and one that parents often value. The chance to be encouraged to see their child in a new light or from a different perspective can have great impact, radically altering the relationship they have with their child.

The first session

The context in which a child arrives in therapy can be viewed as a narrative. Within this narrative is carried an implicit message communicating something of the child's circumstances and personal struggle, if the therapist is willing and able to look for it. As with the referral process, the initial impressions a therapist may have of a child, and the dialogue that subsequently unfolds in the first session, are also part of that narrative.

Unlike an adult arriving at a first privately arranged session with a therapist, a child can never arrive without *some* outside information. There is always a third party involved, and often a fourth or fifth, such as parent, school, social worker, foster carer, and so on. All of these involved parties may influence the first session through the information or consent they provide, or, alternatively, may choose to withhold. The challenge for the existential therapist, if they are to be truly phenomenological, is not to bracket this information and put it aside, but to reflect on how these details make them feel. What emotions come up for them prior to, and during, these first encounters? Do they experience anger at the punitive language of a frustrated teacher? Are they moved by the tragic circumstances described by the social worker? Do they empathize with the struggles of an overwhelmed parent? All of these emotional responses reveal something of the therapist themselves, but also of the world of the child. What must it be like for this child to have to face the teacher every day in school when they induce such an angry response in the therapist? When presented with such information, the assumptions and emotional responses of the therapist become an inescapable part of the child's narrative and cannot be cast aside.

Finally, when the therapist first meets the child and they either fulfil or contradict (or probably a mixture of the two) their assumptions, these surprises, too, can be of value. If existential psychotherapy with children aims to minimize the impact of speculative theory, then often the only reliable source of information the therapist can draw upon is, indeed, how *they* feel when they are with a child. It is important, therefore, that the therapist notices any surprises that may unexpectedly strike them during their first meeting with a child. If the child is described during the referral or assessment process as being wild and uncontrollable, it is important to consider why they do not demonstrate this same behaviour when meeting with the therapist. It is important to reflect upon what makes these encounters so different, and any contradictions in the therapist's anticipatory assumptions and the reality with which they are faced. What might be revealed about this child who can behave so violently and aggressively at home, but appear so timid and vulnerable during their therapeutic sessions?

David

I was asked to work with David by his social worker, who was particularly concerned about frequent periods of debilitating stomach pain which had prevented him from attending school. He was nine years old and popular amongst his peer group, but it stood out to me that his social worker referred to him as a young man who liked to please everyone. When absent from school and away from his friends, he appeared to be increasingly self-conscious, causing his feelings of anxiety to grow.

I was told how he had been greatly affected by the acrimonious split of his parents, who had been married for the first six years of his life. His parents had been in and out of court since their separation, arguing over periods of contact and each other's suitability to have a residence order granted in their name. Throughout this process, there had been allegations of abuse and domestic violence from both sides, and the court had requested an assessment from social services. During their assessment, they had urged David's parents to seek mediation, but had also become increasingly concerned about his emotional wellbeing. By the time he had been referred to me, his parents had been unable to reach a satisfactory solution and his home life was split inconveniently. David, like so many children, appeared to have become a victim of the bitter feelings of his parents. His life was cleaved in two, not just by the practical divisions of two separate homes, but by the emotional turmoil of needing to keep each world away from the other parent.

I initially arranged to meet with both parents and their respective new partners separately before starting to work with David in a local community clinic. Prior to these meetings, they were sent letters offering appointments. Each parent contacted me by phone to rearrange their appointment time and to request that I meet with them at different, more convenient locations. During these phone calls, both parents enquired about the contact I had made with the other, but made no reference at all to the feelings or circumstance of their son. Both parents were seen individually and both were hesitant about providing consent. David's mother said she did not really believe that psychotherapy was necessary and she saw little need for David to have the chance to talk to someone outside his family. His father wondered if David ". . . might not feel more comfortable seeing someone from his school, you know, a more familiar face." Both parents were anxious to discover if the other had signed consent before they committed to the process themselves. There appeared to be little space for either of them to consider the needs of their son other than as a vessel of communication between the two of them.

When it came to our first session, David was brought ten minutes late by his father, who reassured him that he would be waiting outside. When I asked if he was ready to come into the session, it was noticeable how David looked to his father for an answer, perhaps checking if he had permission to answer or if his father wished to answer on his behalf. Although I made little comment about their lateness to either of them, it was clear this was something that embarrassed David, who was obviously trying his best to make a positive impression on me. He stood nervously until I suggested he sit. He chose not to explore any of the toys or art equipment assembled in the room; the two of us sat quietly. I noticed him glancing over at some pencils in a pot on the table, but when our eyes met he hurriedly looked down as if he had been caught out misbehaving and expected to be told off. "Would you like to draw something?" His response was an enthusiastic nod, but again without the confidence to answer verbally. Before selecting each pencil from the pot he asked my permission, even though I had encouraged him to choose whatever he wanted and draw whatever he chose. As he hesitantly put pencil to paper, he drew a small figure in the middle of the page, just slightly off to one side. He stopped frequently to check again if what he drew was acceptable, looking towards me, seemingly expecting words of disapproval. The figure he had tentatively sketched out, however, was not a human one but that of a small monster with spikes all over its back. It was rather like a dinosaur, but without sharp teeth or the menace of a ferocious animal. The creature stood on a dark grey path that led straight across the centre of the page. In front of the creature David drew a large, thick rectangle, which he later described as a wall. There was no alternative route along the path and the creature was standing there facing this large, impenetrable wall. Around the creature he then drew a circle, initially rather like a bubble, which became increasingly like a cloud or some kind of force field as he circled the monster more and more.

Throughout this session, David was exceptionally polite and compliant, answering each intervention I made without hesitation, often appearing to check with me that I was satisfied with his response. The monster, he told me, was stuck. It was prickly and its appearance put others off from coming too close. He explained that it had to eat people in order to survive, but it did not really want to. He went on to describe a city, lying beyond the wall, which had been built to keep the monster out, and he could see no way through. The monster was alone and starving to death, desperate to break through and find people to eat, but at the same time fearful of the hatred it generated. The creature seemed to be well and truly stuck in its own cloud and the emotionless face seemed to speak volumes about David's own self-hatred. The monster, like David, appeared abandoned and alone, without other monsters or people available for it to relate to. It was noticeable to me that the people it most wanted to be with and needed for its nourishment to survive, it also feared it would destroy.

Even more conspicuous than David's moving and emotive narrative throughout this first session was the way in which he conducted himself. He revealed so much about his world-view in how he related to me, and my attitude throughout was just to remain with David, with his experience. In the nervous and compliant way in which he conducted himself, he avoided the possibility of conflict. Conflict, it seemed, had become so familiar in his world and was a burden he carried for all his family. Despite the inability of both his parents to overcome their hurt and grievances, it was he who had ended up being referred for therapy. He existed in a world of tension and fear, one of apprehension and impending gloom. Despite the turmoil that was so familiar to him, it was apparent that David felt alone in this world, and that his own image, like that of the monster, was almost unapproachable and potentially dangerous to those around him. To begin with, he could not bear to express his pain and certainly not in front of me, with the risk of my disapproval. Each meeting we had was an opportunity to co-create new ways to be together. It was clear that what was missing for David was the chance to relate to another: the chance for someone else, for however short a time, to cross over into his world and live alongside him. As our work together progressed, he allowed me closer to him, slowly revealing small aspects of who he was, how he felt, and who he could choose to be. We journeyed together, but, crucially, not always with his polite and compliant acceptance. True progress came when he was not only able to express his own pain and anxiety, but when he felt able to show his anger and frustrations at me, for this importantly demonstrated his willingness to risk conflict and, most importantly, to tolerate the outcomes.

The relationship

Existential psychotherapy places as much, if not more, value on process than on content. What a child says during a session does not carry greater significance than how it is said and what is implicitly revealed in the saying. Sometimes, it is, in fact, the contradictions between the two that are most revealing and help to further the therapist's understanding. Key to experiencing this process is the relationship, and it is this that must be the starting point for the therapist when working with a child. Existential therapy looks first at the relationship, not the individual. There is no control located within the internal world, but an intersubjective relatedness which creates possibilities and, hence, choice.

From an analytic perspective, greater significance is given to the *transference* within a therapeutic relationship, in which feelings are previously constructed and stored, only to be transferred on to the therapist unconsciously. The therapist may then be able to explore this through their own countertransference, projected into them by their relationship with the client's personality (Klein, 1932). For the analyst, we can see there are the superficial, surface relationship and also the true relationship, brought about through processes of transference, countertransference, and projective identification. For the existential psychotherapist, each unique encounter with a child will, of course, be greatly informed by their past experiences and relationships, but these are not present in an internal, covert reality. What occurs is the co-creation of a new relationship in the context of the child's being-in-the-world. The child, as we know, can never exist in isolation and without being-with-others, and this new relationship offers an opportunity to understand and define them in a particular situation. Despite the reality of only the exterior relationship, there is still the intention of clarification of the experience for the child. The relationship presents them with choices, but also the prospect for insight and understanding, developed from awareness of feelings and emotions.

If we are to take the relationship as the starting point of any existential psychotherapy, we can then see that this is no different if the client is an adult or a child. Crucially, the "primordial" existential relatedness of being adds to the importance of the developmental process. A child's growth into adolescence and then adulthood are processes that cannot take place in isolation. A rejected child will often seek security, showing how the other can provide safety for the child's own sense of self. Within the therapeutic relationship, it is important that both parties are open to a true experiential encounter in which the child is eventually able to see the therapist as an individual person and not simply a professional. As each child develops greater understanding of the relationship that has been established through the context of therapy, they may then become aware of their own choices, responsibilities, and, ultimately, their freedom. As a seven-year-old child once said to me during our concluding session together, ". . . to begin with I thought you were just a grown up, but then I learnt we could play together."

CHAPTER FOUR

Play

"Child analysis of whatever school is built around the child's playing."
". . . It is play that is universal, and belongs to health"

(Winnicott, 1971, pp. 39, 41)

Play is an activity viewed by Winnicott as a form of growth. A healthy, growing child will need to play, and Winnicott also claims within his book, *Playing and Reality* (1971), that in monitoring a child's mental health and wellbeing, it is almost possible to disregard all other social dysfunctions if they are able to play creatively. His premise appears to be largely founded upon the importance of play as a facilitator and catalyst for the forming of relationships. He asserts that these relationships, with other people and the child's world around them, fall into categories of being healthy or unhealthy. The emphasis that play makes on the health of these relationships is in communication, and Winnicott suggests psychotherapy is, in some ways, just a specialized and advanced form of communication through playing. The play, in this case, simply aids communication between the two parties.

Play is something deliberate in which we are able to lose ourselves. It is a shared experience in a psychotherapeutic relationship in which I am able either to observe the child I am working with or engage with them. It can be a method of communication, a language if you will, but it does not require interpretation, only hearing. The importance of play in the therapeutic relationship rests with the therapist being able to listen to the play and not fall into patterns of the syntheses of judgements, predictions, and categorizations. If we are really able to engage with the play of children, in a genuine and not a contrived way, either in observing them or through our own active participation, then it is possible to become active players ourselves.

An existential perspective on play

Existentially, play is not merely an activity that should be considered separately from a child. It is not appropriate to notice the child and the play activities in which they are engaged as distinct entities. When entering into imaginative play, the child and therapist do not retain their former, "real" identities, perhaps neatly folded or hung up in a metaphorical cupboard. They are simply the roles they have become. In other words, they are essentially in the moment, and the character or world of that instant is the only one that exists.

When in different contexts in all our lives, we instinctively act in different ways. With my manager at work, I may behave in a professional manner, with my mother, I may try to be dutiful, with my partner and children, affectionate, and so on. These ways of connecting and relating will obviously vary from one occasion to another and are certainly not fixed, but they are all disclosive of my world-view and my being. All of these different ways of relating are "me". They are all who I am at any given moment, and no one way of being is more *me* than any other. Conversely, I may wish that one of these ways of relating is a truer reflection of who I am, a means of self-interpretation and an identity to retain, but it is not.

A frequently coiled rope may retain within its structure a desire to return to its established pattern, even when pulled out of shape, or forced into an alternative pattern. It appears to retain a true shape or be taken to adopt a false shape. This shape, however, is not an inherent part of its makeup. The natural tendency of the rope to repeat its experience and adopt the familiar is similar to tendencies that exist in all of us, and children are by no means exempt from this. It is important to note, however, that the desire and comfort found in returning to familiar patterns does not demonstrate the existence of a core or *true* self, more real than any other. As with a child's play, each character they adopt is representative of them in that moment. In so far as a child's play provides a key to their life, it is because in their play is projected their manner of being towards the world, that is, towards time and others (Merleau-Ponty, 2002, p.183).

Play as communication

Play may also become important as a means for communication between two people. Young children will ordinarily not have a large vocabulary to choose from for their communication, and in the forming of their relationships. This is particularly important in psychotherapy, for two reasons. First, the expression of emotional experience could be said to be an integral, core element to the therapeutic process itself. Second, the therapeutic relationship into which the child is thrown will develop only through dialogue. Play and creativity are inherent in the realization of both.

Although children may have a somewhat reduced emotional lexicon from which to operate, they are more readily able to express themselves in the language of play. Prior to writing about a child that he saw during a session, Winnicott proposed that it was hardly necessary ". . . to illustrate something so obvious as playing". However, I believe that playing is, in many aspects as a means of communication and experience, something that has been forgotten or become limited by most adults. Winnicott assumes that play is in some way obvious, but, as adults, we almost disregard it and, indeed, forget what it is in our daily lives. Certainly, within modern society, it seems to me that little time in the life of the average adult is put aside for playing, and the pastimes of our society that dictate a purpose and product have become the elements that predominate.

To be lost in play . . .

The philosopher Hans-Georg Gadamer wrote about the importance of play, suggesting that the player is aware that they are playing within a world that is normally determined by "the seriousness of purpose". However, although the player may know that they are playing, they do not know what *it* is. As he wrote, ". . . above all, what no longer exists is the world, in which we live as our own" (2000, p. 101).

For Gadamer, it is important that we are able to lose ourselves in some way for an experience to be considered play. We must know that we are about to play, and must take it seriously for it to be effective; nevertheless it is more than just the communication between two people that Winnicott talks of. To illustrate his thoughts, Gadamer used the example of art:

> If, in connection with the experience of art, we speak of play, this refers neither to the attitude, nor even to the state of mind of the creator or of those enjoying the work of art, nor to the freedom of a subjectivity expressed in play, but to the mode of being of the work of art itself. [*ibid.*, p. 91]

Here, Gadamer uses the example of art in order to illustrate that it is the work of art itself that becomes something new. Art is an example of play because it serves no direct purpose; although a painting may have aesthetic value, it does not bring us food or money unless we are professional artists. Art, in this case, has a danger that it could become something else, although it is never real, but only a representation or expression. However, most importantly, we must recognize the mode of being of something that is not real but, at the same time, undertaken in seriousness and entered into wholeheartedly, and often with passion. The significance Gadamer gave to play is noticeable in his proposal that play is not serious, but has its own "sacred seriousness".

Jack

I believe, when working therapeutically with children, that it is important to treat them with the same respect that we would perhaps assume with adult client work or relationships. This is something so simple, which may often be forgotten by many professionals working with children in health, education, and social care. This is also true of engaging in play. If the therapist is always looking in at the play from an objective viewpoint, interpreting and diagnosing, they are unable to relate wholeheartedly. Play should not be considered as secondary to any other way of relating.

Jack was ten years old, attending a mainstream, inner-city school. He was diagnosed as having dyslexia shortly before being referred to me. He lived with his mother and sister, who suffered frequent discomfort and pain from a severe physical disability. His mother believed he might have found it distressing and even traumatic to witness his sister's often violent fits, and to live with doubt and unpredictability each time she was rushed to hospital. He had already attended therapy sessions at a London hospital some time before I started seeing him, and his previous class teacher, who had begun to become concerned, referred him to me for therapeutic support again. The initial reasons for the referral focused predominantly on his confidence, or, rather, lack of it, which was affecting many aspects of his life, both in school and in his world beyond. His mother hoped he would be able to express himself with greater self-assurance. Jack had told me he wanted to find his voice. We agreed to meet at his school, in a small room separate from the main classrooms.

Jack had a very depressed look about his general appearance. He spoke very quietly and, particularly at the start of our work together, I found it difficult to understand him when he spoke. His teacher described Jack as often on the fringe of activities and, although not really bullied, he did not appear to have any stable and consistent friends. At the outset of our work together, Jack almost always looked down. He appeared to be ashamed in many ways of who he was. The threat of his sister leaving to go to hospital at any moment was real and present. Every day he lived with challenge and potential guilt from being healthy and able-bodied, compared to his sister. In many ways, he chose to hide away from the world and diminish his own presence. Initially, it felt uncomfortable to be with Jack, as he perhaps felt uncomfortable to be himself. My role quickly became one of engagement, trying to form an acceptable bridge to Jack that did not present an overwhelming fear of rejection. Allowing him space to play without judgement was a vital step to his personal growth and self-acceptance. Judgement, alongside splits of good and bad, continued, however, to become recurrent themes in his play. But, as I frequently reminded myself, he felt confident enough to play and, importantly, to lose himself on occasion in fantastically elaborate narratives.

After eighteen sessions he appeared to have begun to slowly grow in confidence within the therapy room: his speech was clearer and more audible, on occasion he laughed and smiled, and his play became more creative and less inhibited. Within his narrative, the theme of good battling against evil had become prevalent and began to recur. Below is an account of the playful narrative that developed within our nineteenth session together.

> Jack seemed very lively when he first came to the session. I collected him from class and he was skipping through the corridors and into the room. He entered before me and turned on the heater himself, which he had not, to my recollection, done before. He sat down for a second; I followed his lead, but he quickly stood up again and took down two wooden toy farm buildings and a bag of plastic toy animals. He aligned the two farm buildings on the table and then emptied out the entire bag of animals in a large pile. He began standing them up and placing them on the table, more or less in the positions in which they fell, except one dog (the dog had bright red eyes, and I thought to myself that it looked somewhat scary). He placed the dog on the edge of the table on his own, away from the other animals.
>
> *Me*: He looks alone.
>
> *Jack*: Yes, that's because he's evil.
>
> [Jack paused for a minute, appearing to think about what he was saying.]
>
> *Me*: What makes him evil?
>
> *Jack*: Just is . . . [He continued to place all the animals upright on the table. As this carried on, I noticed that they were all being placed into groups of their own kind: all the cows together, all the pigs, all the ducks, etc. I assisted him in finishing the process of standing up all the animals, which took a few minutes. During this time he also selected a black bull, which he placed next to the "evil" dog, on the edge of the table.]

Jack: Now you can be the evil ones . . .

[He gestured to the evil animals, which were closer to me, on my side of the table.]

. . . and you have to try and kill my ones.

[I decided to move the two animals I had been given towards the larger group. As I began to do this, Jack moved most of the animals back into the house, although a small group stayed outside. Jack chose a horse, much larger than many of the other animals, which jumped on to the two evil ones and kicked them back.]

Jack: Now they are dead.

Me: What happens to them now?

[Reflecting on how the animals were, was intended to bring about an increased awareness in his emotional being. Jack found it difficult to verbalize his own emotions and to express himself in relation to other people. The concept of death, which he had introduced himself, seemed to make this an appropriate opportunity for us to explore the possibilities of how others may, or, indeed, may not feel within his narrative. Until this point in the session, I feel that I had simply been accompanying him on his journey of creative expression, which I hoped would not be interrupted. Jack chose, however, to respond verbally on a more pragmatic note. Similar to much of his behaviour, though, the relative brevity of his response made it difficult to know how he understood the intervention in terms of his emotional experience. This unknowing is, however, to be managed by the therapist and the challenge lies in resisting the attraction of speculation and further objective analysis.]

Jack: It's OK, they can come back to life, immediately . . .

Me: Immediately?

Jack: Yeah, they're OK now . . .

[Then the other animals in the small group that was outside the house, about seven or eight in total, continued to jump on the two evil animals. This process was performed repeatedly, and every time they were close, they would knock the evil animals back, sometimes quite fiercely, throwing them off the table.]

Me: There seems to be a lot of fighting and some animals look very angry to me.

Jack: Yes, I know . . .

[As Jack said these words, he took a large gorilla and two lions down from a nearby shelf and put them on the table on the side of the good animals. These new animals were able to jump around easily. The play focused mainly on the gorilla, which was able to kill the two evil animals, perhaps with even greater ease and efficiency than the farm animals previously.]

Jack: Now their owner's come back, and she's got her baby and collected it from school and here's its pram . . . and here's its cot.

[As Jack said this, he chose additional toy figures from a box nearby and placed them on the table.]

[He killed the evil animals again, this time with the woman; he pushed them back behind a barrier which he had made, or behind one of the farm houses.]

Jack: Whack! Whack! You naughty animals, chasing everyone around the farm.

[This was said quite loudly. And the woman continued to kill them, eventually using a small plastic sign that he had taken from one of the farm buildings to hit them over the head with.]

Me: How do you think they feel while they are being hit? I wonder what that's like?

Jack: Don't know.

[He shrugged his shoulders.]

Me: Do you think they deserve to be hit so much?

Jack: Yes, they are evil.

[He took a small plastic teddy bear, which was the smallest toy that could obviously be seen in the room. He was straight away placed on the side of the good animals, and appeared able to defeat the other animals with ease, despite his size.]

Jack: He can defeat everyone. He's the greatest.

[After a while, the teddy bear seemed to move around the table a great deal with the much larger gorilla.]

Me: Are they friends?

[Here, my aim was to encourage Jack again to reflect on the nature of the relationships involved in the play, perhaps to experience how the bear felt; whether it felt alone or together. I was hoping that Jack might reflect upon how the characters were relating to each other. This question was responded to swiftly, however, and he soon moved the narrative along to a different scenario, again choosing not to verbalize anything beyond a practical answer and the continuation of his narrative. This statement is not, of course, intended to belittle the importance of this creative play.]

Jack: Yes, they met at the zoo and now they are friends.

[The bear was moved to the other side of the table and was then hidden in a chest, away from the other animals.]

Me: Where is the bear?

[This was said as narrative, not as a direct question.]

Jack: Now it's seven hundred thousand years later, and the lady has turned into an old lady.

[He took hold of a figure of an old lady and just threw the other lady away, over his shoulder.]

Jack: Where's the bear? Oh, here he is . . . yeah . . . I've found my bear.

[The small bear reappeared and flew around very triumphantly. Jack stood up quite abruptly and said that the game was finished. This quite startled me, as he stopped in the middle of an action and finished so suddenly without any external interruption, and seemingly without any ending. As he said this, he instantly started packing away all of the toys that he had put out on the table.]

[His next activity seemed to be more light-hearted, taking Jack away from the magnitude and experience of his previous narrative. The story had ended abruptly, and Jack appeared to find lighter relief in talking on a toy plastic telephone that was in the room. Children should be able to set their own pace in the session, and there is also obviously some therapeutic experience to be taken from the subsequent lighter dialogue.]

Jack: Let's use the phones.

[He picked up the two plastic toy telephones and put them on the table.]

Me: OK.

[We each rang the phone, and then both picked up; I spoke first.]

Me: Who's there?

[No answer.]

Me: Is that Jack?

Jack: Yes, hello.

[There then followed a quick succession of calls in which we asked each other, mainly, who was there and how we were. I recall Jack asked me to deliver something to his house. During the conversations there was more of a frivolous and lighter atmosphere, and Jack even laughed a few times as the conversations became more jovial. I reminded him that the time for our session was nearly over, and he asked if we could play a game of catch with some rubber balls before we completely finished: this had become something of a common ending ritual. I explained how we only had time for a quick game, during which I asked how he was. He seemed to think for a while, not answering straight away, but later said, "OK".]

[Towards the end of this session I felt more comfortable in allowing myself to adopt a lighter approach to the dialogue between us. This was an important factor because of the solemn nature of Jack's creation and telling of the narrative. This provided him with the option of being another way in the therapy room, not having to be serious. It was also important to allow Jack time to reflect upon the session. This was often carried out during a ball game, in which he felt able to speak quite candidly and allow himself time to process his thoughts before having to return to the classroom.]

The power and importance of play requires a serious commitment. There appears to be value in losing ourselves in the narrative, generating powerful emotional content and allowing each child opportunities to explore different avenues and create possibilities. This session with Jack reveals the therapist's personal challenge in moving in and out of a wholehearted faithfulness and engagement in the play. At times, it can be impossible to not be aware that the play is, in a sense, not real, and, as such, can be viewed and understood as observing audience. During other moments, the therapist can become enveloped in the play, and it becomes the only real world. Reflected within the play is how a child experiences and relates to other people and, ultimately, to the world. It can be a privilege to be invited in to share this play world and, significantly, to observe the points at which a child may move in and out of engaging with me explicitly and directly, or putting me in the position of observing audience watching the narrative unfold.

Above all, the narrative should not be interpreted through a detailed exegesis, analysing each choice or characterization, but understood by allowing the message of the play to be revealed through a process of hermeneutic understanding. This idea is not a new one in therapy and beyond: the role of creative narrative in theatre has, for example, been used many times, and as far back as the work of Aeschylus and the ancient Greeks. We can see, in the example of *Hamlet*, how Shakespeare uses the instrument of a play within his play to illustrate the emotional detail of the context of the characters in the audience and their relationships. The play itself does not need to be analysed in detail or grammatically or dramatically dissected to see the message it conveys. It is ontologically revealing, disclosing the context of the play's main protagonists. In the soliloquy delivered by Hamlet immediately following the play, he reflects, bemused, on the emotional response of Polonius to the recounting of the death of Priam;

> "O, what a rogue and peasant slave am I!
> Is it not monstrous that this player here,
> But in fiction, in a dream of passion,
> Could force his soul so to his own conceit
> That from her working all his visage wanned,
> Tears in his eyes, distraction in his aspect,
> A broken voice, and his whole function suiting
> With forms to his conceit? And all for nothing."
> [Shakespeare, 1980, 2.II: 547–554]

We can see, here, that if the audience is responsive and open to the disclosure of the narrative, its message and the emotional content are realized in an experience even more powerful than explicit dialogue.

CHAPTER FIVE

Family and method

Even when a child is abandoned or orphaned, they always exist in relation to others, most significantly their family. The infant being with her mother is primordially constitutive of its very existence. There is never an infant without a mother. In psychotherapy, for many adult clients attending sessions, a discussion of their memories and understanding of their childhood and their family relationships are commonplace. For a child, the influence of their family is inescapable. It is important to consider, however, at least in a brief manner, what is really understood by the term "family".

The word "family" can be used in two main contexts: as a primary social group, or in the biological sense as a categorization of animals into taxonomic groups. Importantly, the first meaning is imbued with the notion that its function is to provide for its members, while the second signifies that commonality can be found between its members: that is to say, the criteria for being classified in that particular way, for example, Felidae (cat family) as opposed to Canidae (dog family). From an existential perspective, however, the family should be seen as a specific context in which the relationships between each member can be highlighted. If being-in-the-world always essentially means being-with-others, then family is no exception to this, and the abstract concept of a unique individual existing in isolation should be abandoned. The child always exists with their own distinctive history and their family environment, but an opportunity to transcend their context through awareness of choices and possibilities is still achievable. If, on the contrary, the family is seen as a system or a whole object, then it can become viewed as an organism in its own right, with its own "pathology" or patterns of behaviour. The family should be seen as an intrinsic part of the being-with, relational existence of the child.

Michael

Throughout the day, Michael's hands shook uncontrollably, a clear repercussion of the terrible abuse inflicted upon him over many years. Now aged fourteen and growing into a young man, the shaking of his hands was something I found even more alarming. It alarmed me greatly because of the normality of this in his life. His hands shook and he accepted this as part of his living being. It had become a necessity for him, like breathing.

I was told by Michael's social worker how he had been sexually abused by his biological father and, from time to time, locked in a small cupboard if he protested too vehemently or his behaviour was too disruptive. He was subsequently placed with foster carers, who, it was alleged, had also abused him further, and this had led to a string of unsuccessful placements. When I met him to offer therapeutic sessions, he was living in a residential children's home a long way from his original family. Yet, it was clear that Michael's family remained close to him in so many ways. For Michael, the way he related to his family had become a demonstrable part of who he was.

A family, thus, can be viewed fundamentally as a context informing the way a child is, and, as with language, should not be considered as an objectified concept. As a context, it should be understood as helping to create a history or perception through which the child lives their life. The therapist must consequently not seek to analyse and deconstruct the family as a system, but to uncover the context, broadening it ever wider to create possibilities.

We can see, therefore, from an existential perspective, that the family is part of the child's being-with-others and part of their world.

Method

The "uncovering", or opening up, of the child's perception of their family should not be seen as a method for analysis, however. In order to develop greater awareness of the choices and possibilities a child faces, it is essential for the therapist to look at the relationships of which the child is a part through awareness of the phenomena. If this type of circumspective interpretation is reduced to a set of techniques and methods, then the interpretation of the relationship can only be understood in one way. In effect, all else is lost.

The etymology of the word "method" lies in the Greek language, and could be separated into the two composites of *meta,* meaning after, and *hodos,* meaning way. "After-way" begins to hint at something that can be repeated. This etymological definition alludes not just to the way by which things may be carried out, but also what occurs after, which is a duplication of the original way. We are talking, then, of something that could be systematically presented or taught. This repeatability is somewhat forgotten in the more modern understanding of "method" as a way of doing something. It is, by its nature, orderly and scientific. Palmer writes,

> Method is an effort to measure and control from the side of the interpreter; it is the opposite of letting the phenomenon lead. The openness of "experience"—which alters the interpreter himself from the side of the text—is antithetical to method. Thus method is in reality a form of dogmatism, separating the interpreter from the work, standing between it and him, and barring him from experiencing the work in its fullness. Analytical seeing is blindness to experience; it is analytical blindness. [1969, p. 247]

This extract is taken from a book in which Palmer refers to the difference between hermeneutics and the analytical interpretation of literature, but within psychotherapeutic realms there seems to exist this same dichotomy of knowledge and experience. As Palmer suggests that the "phenomenon should lead", he does not exclude the interpreter, who is very much involved in an active process. This passage tells us that the "analyst" is separated or removed from the work, and that analysis stands in the way of experience. A tendency exists today to define experience in a way that is completely orientated toward scientific knowledge and does not so much take into account a personal, inner historicity of experience. Science aims to make everything objective and verifiable, and this, ultimately, may lead to the claim that only what is verifiable is real. Lying open to experiencing a piece of literature, or, indeed, a relationship with a child in its fullness, does in some way require a knowledge, but this is not a scientific knowledge that offers a position of theoretical safety.

From this stance, there lies the danger in being told too much about a child, and of the opinions of other members of their family or the professionals working around them. This knowledge can be taken as complete scientific fact, provoking huge assumptions and prejudices. Even the knowledge that a particular child is attending regular sessions with a psychotherapist can provoke powerful reactions. It is common for one sibling to be brought to see a therapist by their parents having been already identified as the problem. It becomes crucially important for the therapist to be able to look at the whole picture, as indispensable information is disclosed in the parent's selection of one sibling over another for needing therapeutic support.

Sean

I am reminded of the mother of a young boy named Sean. He was an extremely anxious boy, highlighted to our service by an education welfare worker for having such a poor record of attendance at school. My first response was to arrange a meeting to challenge his mother on why he missed school so frequently and what difficulties lay behind this. Upon meeting Sean's mother, it quickly became evident that his anxiety was not about being at school, but more about being away from his mother at home. She described to me how she had been sexually abused over many years throughout her childhood by a relative. When she finally felt able to make this known to the rest of her family, it emerged that her sister was also abused by the same man. She remembered, shortly after this disclosure, being referred by their family doctor to be assessed by a clinical psychologist, while her sister was referred for counselling. This was a distinct difference that had stayed with her over many years. She understood this distinction as implying that she was unable to cope as well as her sister and required a greater degree of specialist input. Her own perception of the difference between a counsellor and a psychologist acted to encourage her to identify as more of a victim than her sister. This was to have an impact that had not only affected her for many years, but now also had repercussions for her son.

The problems of methodology

Much modern psychotherapy practised with children continues towards a scientific tradition of objectification and interpretation. The experience of the interpreter is unimportant or lost. The psychotherapist who is working psychodynamically, for example, may hope that by the naming of objective internal processes and by trying to understand them from within their own dynamic terms, some new meaning may emerge. In this case, the child's presentation could become like a book that has been the target of many questions, perhaps enquiring into the author's pathology or infant experiences, and the therapist a reader who has not tried to understand the question that a book has put to them. A reader who is not relying on method will remain open to understanding the question that is behind a text, the question that brought the text into being. As with a literary interpretation, the therapist must develop the art of listening and hearing, for this could lead to an openness for learning that cannot be anticipated or foreseen. What methodology seems to forget is experience, and, within this, the involvement of two parties in a dialectic.

The philosopher Hans-Georg Gadamer focused in his writing on awareness being raised through experience. He appeared to share the view of Hegel that experience is an encounter of raising awareness from dialogue. In *Truth and Method* (Wahrheit und Methode), Gadamer quotes Hegel, saying, "[There is a] movement in which awareness practices on both its knowing and its object; insofar as, for it, a new object is generated out of this, that is truly to be called 'experience'" (2000, p. 195).

Here, we can see a reversal that includes the "knower", who becomes incorporated into a process that commences with an idea of disturbance. The object that one has experienced is not as had been expected; it has been viewed in a new light and is changed. We, as the knower, are then ourselves changed by virtue of knowing the object differently. The personal experience of the psychotherapist within their child–therapist relationships reveals to us something new, and in order for this to take place, they must be open to the possibilities that lie in not knowing in a manner that is concrete and fixed. The experience that is relevant here is not a scientific, objectifiable knowledge of information, but is something I consider to be closer to our everyday use of the word "wisdom". Palmer (1969, pp. 195–196) gives the example of a man who has dealt with people all his life, and, while his experience cannot be called objectifiable knowledge, he has acquired some knowledge of the way things are that cannot be classified or conceptualized—it is more a "knowledge of people".

Many parents bring their children to therapy expecting answers, and, with concerning regularity, expecting them from me. This creates for me a personal dilemma of wanting the children to keep on coming to see me and engaging in a process, but also at the same time feeling that if I am going to be honest to them, part of this process involves both parents and child becoming aware, implicitly or explicitly, that I do not have *answers* to give.

The existential psychotherapist John Heaton once said to me, "I can't tell you something that you don't already know about yourself, but I can encourage a different perspective" (personal communication, 2003).

Part of the dilemma lies in my own anxiety that this may not be enough for many parents or families and the position this puts me in. Perhaps this is not necessarily in itself knowledge the therapist possesses, but merely an advantage of having more confidence in the face of not knowing than the clients, whatever their age. However, even as I write this, I am not sure. An answer to this predicament may not rest with a rule of truth, but from turning towards personal experiences of play and humility.

Self-disclosure is an example of an area within psychotherapy that could be seen to contain humility for the therapist. Through disclosure, the therapist becomes less of an abstract professional and more vulnerable to emotional engagement with the child before them. It is even true to say that in disclosure that is felt to be judgemental or critical by the child, the therapist becomes vulnerable to an unpredictable shift from whatever may have preceded. In truthful disclosure, the therapist brings their involvement to the attention of the child and is not able to hide behind theory and objectification.

This calls to mind an article by Van Deurzen (1995). She began as follows, under the heading of "Theoretical aspects",

> I have learnt much, first of all from Kierkegaard (Kierkegaard 1844, 1846), who represents to me the never-ending battle with existential anxiety. Reading him inevitably reminds me of the importance of starting from the core of insecurity in oneself. How crucial it is to keep discovering again and again that one is nothing, that one is only emptiness, that one is non-substantial and that nothing is ever given for keeps nor can be taken for granted—not one's possessions, not one's character, not one's achievements or anything else in the world. [1995, p. 9]

When reading this passage, I become aware of the humility present, not only in the thoughts of Van Deurzen, but also in the work of Kierkegaard himself. Subsequent to this passage, she goes on to suggest that this position is perhaps the first step to questioning and the realization that ". . . the essence of being human is to not have an essence". This, for Van Deurzen, represents an opportunity for becoming open to discovering new possibilities, possibilities which are not prepared by someone else. This also represents somehow the humility of Kierkegaard's work: he does not proffer answers, but merely places the reader who is willing to go at the start of a journey from which possibilities may be revealed.

If this humility from reading Kierkegaard (which is something that I feel I have experienced myself) was inherent in the relationship between therapist and child, then the therapist would be able to include mutuality and humbleness in their sessions and not have to rely on scientific knowledge, but could, instead, rely on his or her historicity and wisdom.

Jimmy

Jimmy attended a small village primary school close to a large community of the Irish traveller culture. His close family had been settled on the site for some time, and his extended family even longer. When his mother had finally chosen to enrol him in school, it came as a dramatic shock to Jimmy, who was more used to working with his father or playing out among the trailers. He was ten years old, and had only ever spent, cumulatively, up to a few months being educated at school throughout his entire life.

The lifestyle of Jimmy's family had meant they had rarely remained settled long enough for him to form any relationships from outside the traveller community, let alone send him to school. Both his parents said they valued education up to a certain age, but they were both illiterate and Jimmy's father worked away on a seasonal basis for long periods of the year.

When I came to meet Jimmy, it was at school and he was immediately recognizable. He was a large boy with short red hair and freckles. He wore a white T-shirt and ill-fitting trousers. It was noticeable that he did not wear socks, and immediately obvious that he was certainly unaccustomed to school uniform. He looked to me as though the school building itself was a confinement for him, but he greeted me for the first time with a broad grin and a firm handshake.

Jimmy had been referred by his headteacher, who was concerned at his violent outbursts. He had only been in the school for a short time, and the staff had already found his behaviour difficult to manage. He struggled with the most basic of academic tasks and the whole environment was a threatening challenge for him. He had become anxious around the school, often walking out of class, retreating to a quiet corner, or quickly provoking a violent confrontation with a classmate. His teacher described to me a developing pattern in which Jimmy might feel challenged by something new, and, without the skills or experience to approach it with conviction, he would simply lash out, avoiding the task and returning to the physicality of a more familiar and comfortable violence. Despite these sizeable difficulties, Jimmy seemed determined to spend some time in school, now that he had been enrolled. It had taken a while for Jimmy's mother to agree to the school making a referral to our service, and, once she had given her consent, I agreed to meet with him.

My expectation for our first session was that, despite his initially confident appearance, he would be nervous and need to be reassured. I anticipated he may be reluctant to come to the session, despite having agreed to do so previously, and that he may feel unsafe and leave before the end of our allotted fifty minutes. School was such a strange and foreign place that it seemed almost inevitable Jimmy would find attending therapy sessions an even more perplexing and extraordinary experience. For our first session, however, my assumptions were completely wrong. He was happy to leave his class, attend the session, and, once settled, stay for the complete duration. He presented as confident and chatty, smiling through the session in a way I had not anticipated at all. He was inquisitive and curious, eager to learn about my world and my way of life, which seemed so different to his own. It became evident that our roles had been reversed, and he was the one able to put me at ease and reduce my anxiety. By the end of the session, I felt confident that Jimmy would be happy to return the following week and we would be able to continue to discuss further the purpose of our meetings and how he hoped to use the sessions.

Upon arriving at school the next week, however, I was immediately beckoned into the headteacher's office. She explained how Jimmy had not attended school at all since our previous session, and she had contacted his mother to discuss the matter. His mother had said Jimmy felt the meeting had been "OK" but he had not liked me and did not want to return. I was shocked. I felt things had gone much better than I could have hoped for. Jimmy had agreed to come and meet with me again, but only in the presence of the headteacher, and only for a brief time. During the meeting, he looked down and mumbled much of the time, a stark contrast to the boy I had met just a week before. Initially, he chose not say what it was about me he disliked or why he did not want to come. He then appeared to contradict himself by saying it was not me personally he did not like, but it was "just me". He went on to describe how he had never been alone with an adult before and certainly not a man. He lived as part of a large family, in a tight-knit community where there was always company. Their trailers were positioned very near to each other and Jimmy spent almost all of his time outside, playing with siblings and cousins around the site. Like school, Jimmy said he actually enjoyed the session, but was unable to feel comfortable being in a room with just one other person.

It seemed as if Jimmy had at first chosen to hide his anxiety, and perhaps adopt an air of calm and control during our session so as to put me at ease. He later described how this was motivated largely out of fear, for this was such a new experience for him and he was extremely cautious of how I may react to him. We agreed eventually to build up to the structure of sessions which I had come to expect, primarily compromising by meeting outside his classroom, and later, leaving the door open during our sessions.

Ironically, the boundaries and securities I thought Jimmy would crave in order to feel safer and able to trust me were the actions that threatened him the most. My knowledge and understanding of Jimmy's culture and family background were effectively of no help to me. It was being open to understanding Jimmy himself which enabled our relationship to progress. Before the sessions, I had met him for such a short time and taken many of my expectations from how his schoolteachers had described him. I had used this "knowledge" to construct a plan, which was to try to make him feel at ease, but in a way that was solely built from my own perspective. The methods of therapy had become intrusive, and it was only through allowing myself to engage with Jimmy that we were able to begin to form a trusting relationship.

CHAPTER SIX

Family and context

Existential psychotherapy holds no refuge for the reality of intrapsychic processes. The mind is not the home of the psychological challenges children may face in their life. These are found in the context in which they find themselves, essentially in their world. For the therapist to look at and try to understand these challenges, they must, then, do so not by uncovering internal, "intrapsychic" processes, but through an understanding of each child's context. Traditional analytic thought is anchored by the interplay of individuality and consciousness and it assumes a Cartesian picture of the mind: children are effectively bodies and minds amicably brought together, accepted as givens and explored in a relational sense, not as a whole. The context in which we all find ourselves, however, is one of being in relation to others. The existential therapeutic process, which begins to develop then in light of a perspective of context, involves the opening up of possibilities. Each question or intervention provokes further enquiry, and so on, and so on, in order that any understanding for therapist and child is not reductive and limiting but each meaning creates new meaning. Without internal intrapsychic processes, the search for a "true" reality is meaningless and each phenomenological disclosure speaks to us of the context and the child's relationships.

The most important context for a child is their family, and it is here that existential therapists have previously devoted much of their efforts in understanding the presentations of their clients. We can see, in the pioneering work of Laing and Esterson at the Tavistock clinic, how the family was taken as a starting point for a radical re-evaluation of the understanding of so-called "mental illness". Over a period of five years, prior to the publication of their book, *Sanity, Madness and the Family* (1970), they embarked on a study, working with young women (who had already been given a diagnosis of schizophrenia) and their families. Their work was a departure from the traditional and widespread assumption that when a person is diagnosed with schizophrenia it is because their behaviour is caused by a particular physiological or psychological disturbance, *a thing* called schizophrenia. Even Bleuler (1966), the originator of the term, coining it as a preferable alternative to the previously prevalent and excessively broad "dementia praecox" (effectively, "precocious or early dementia"), did not establish it as an illness or self-contained disease. Laing and Esterson developed a model of engagement with the family as well as the "patient" in an effort to comprehend the circumstances that had led to their current condition or life circumstances.

Laing and Esterson

The most important aspect of their work focused on, as they termed it, *dialectical investigation*. As Esterson reinforces (1972), the importance in understanding the presentations of these women within their families is through uncovering and laying bare the relationships. This is, ultimately, the process of disclosure of the client's world-view and, therefore, of herself.

> In relating, persons experience the situation in a particular way. They experience it as their situation. They relate, they experience themselves relating, they experience the possibility of relating . . . They experience themselves, the relation and that to which they relate. [1972, p. 214]

They were also able to build upon the importance highlighted of dialectical contradictions revealed within families by the "Double-Bind" theory of Bateson, Jackson, Haley, and Weakland (1956). The "patient" diagnosed with schizophrenia is essentially observed being confronted with impossible choices by other members of their family, principally their parents. An example of this can be seen in the description of "the Head" family by Laing and Esterson (1970, p. 180). The study reports interviews conducted with the family following what was described previously as a psychotic breakdown of a "schizophreniform" type suffered by the daughter of the family, Jean. She grew up as part of a household in a strong position of conflict, placing great emphasis on their religious beliefs and, in particular, the notion of humility, trying to live a humble existence. They make reference to the difficulty of a rich man squeezing into heaven, but, at the same time, there is also an expectation and, indeed, praise for the status the family appears to have gained from material success. They have a large house, acting as means of illustration for their success and desire for material gains. Although this is viewed within the study as the backdrop for Jean's experiences of having her decision making controlled by her parents, it also acts as a suitable example of Bateson, Jackson, Haley, and Weakland's theory. Jean is caught in a position of being dammed if she is successful, or letting the family down if she is not.

In their family analysis, Laing and Esterson closely examined two terms they derived from the work of Sartre: "praxis" and "process". *Praxis*, they explain, "refers to events that are the deeds of doers or groups of doers . . . It refers to the acts of an agent". Praxis, then, is the repercussion of deliberate action, whereas *process* refers to "events or a pattern of events of which no doer or agent is the author" (1970, p. 2). Within normal physical illness of the body, they explain, an organism is afflicted by process, which limits or affects its behaviour. If, for example, I was unfortunate enough to badly break my leg in many places, it may be unlikely that I am subsequently able to walk until the breaks have healed. This is because the leg would simply be unable to support the weight of my body. This is due to process. The accident may originally have been caused by my own choices and deliberate decisions, such as choosing to make a parachute jump without sufficient training or preparation. This is praxis.

Throughout *The Leaves of Spring* (a thorough examination of one of the families in their initial studies), Esterson argues that the Danzig family developed a confusion between behaviour they attributed to either praxis or process. His thesis was based on the ensuing disorientation that grew out of these patterns of contradiction. The behaviour of the young woman within the family, diagnosed as being schizophrenic, was ascribed wrongly to process and not to the outcome of her own deliberate and autonomous decisions. Her parents frequently contradicted themselves during the interviews, fretting and complaining that she would not dedicate herself to anything. They said she had cast aside their conservative and orthodox religious beliefs, and then criticized her for reading the bible late at night over long periods of time. This behaviour they attributed to the eccentricities of her "illness". Throughout the book there are many examples of behaviour they chose to attribute to illness, and, as Esterson claims, began to develop a family praxis. They outwardly purported to espouse certain values and beliefs, but, implicitly within the family, they had agreed to function to an alternative set of principles. Their "ill" daughter, Sarah, was, however, often excluded from these implicit agreements and subsequently ostracized for her responses both in public and, it seemed, in private. She was viewed as embarrassing by the rest of the family because she did not conform to their contradictions.

Stadlen and Stadlen (2005) highlight the presupposition of many studies prior to the work of Laing and Esterson, including Bateson, Jackson, Haley, and Weakland (1956), by perceiving schizophrenia as an illness. Even today, these theories are considered in some psychiatric circles as peripheral, due to their emphasis on the social nature of schizophrenia, and especially the family as a contributing factor. Laing and Esterson built upon and progressed an alternative tradition, through their detailed analysis of the communication of whole family interviews. Notably, these were neither just family observations nor interviews conducted with the clients/patients alone. It is the detailed analysis of the family communication that revealed the contradictions. These inconsistencies within the families placed the daughters (diagnosed as schizophrenic) in untenable existential positions. Fundamentally, our sense of who we are, our sense of being, our "ontological security", emerges from the intrinsic fact that we are always being-with-others. If the others closest to us, those who bring us into the world, influencing our very existence, that is, our family, provide such unstable and conflicting messages, then difficulties are almost inevitable.

Danny

Danny was described on his referral form as an extremely violent young boy who wanted to make friends and work with his peers, but was unable to. His school wrote that he was "aware he is different from his peers but unsure how to control his temper or how to relate to others". Danny had recently been permanently excluded from his previous school following an incident in which he was physically restrained by his headteacher and had ended up punching her in the face. He was seven years old. When referred to our service, he had been attending a new school for just a few weeks, and the staff there, too, were already struggling to manage his behaviour.

When I first met Danny's parents, they appeared equally keen and desperate for support. His mother told me how she, in particular, had struggled to manage him from a young age and how this had been compounded by a sequence of rejections. Relatives had refused to have him round at their house, and he had been asked to leave several nurseries because of his behaviour. His mother had been forced to give up work to care for him before he was old enough to attend school, and this had left the whole family increasingly socially isolated. By the time Danny was able to attend infant school, even before entering the school gates, his family had been asked if he could start on a partial timetable. When he was in school, for just a few mornings a week, Danny spent almost all of his time at the back of the class being educated alone and constantly monitored by a teaching assistant. His parents were now expecting another child, and had no idea how they would be able to attend to a newborn baby given the amount of time and attention Danny appeared to demand.

His father was a large, athletic man who adopted a strict "no nonsense" approach to parenting. Danny was kept, both metaphorically and sometimes literally, on a tight leash by his parents. He was not allowed to watch cartoons on television, in case he became too excited or was exposed to violent messages. In short, he was given no freedom at all at home and was, consequently, sent a clear message that he could not be trusted and could not care for himself.

Danny faced a huge challenge in coming to terms with his own identity. He had been diagnosed with Aspergers Syndrome and ADHD. Both at home and throughout much of his educational experiences, he had also been confronted with huge contradictions. He was constantly criticized for his actions and behaviours, for which he had suffered and been punished from almost the first time he attended nursery. On the other hand, he was told by his parents and through his diagnoses that he was unable to control his behaviour and consequently was not allowed to watch television or play computer games like his peers. At the same time, he was criticized both at school and home for being unsociable and unable to play with other children. He was even "told off" when he struggled to be able to do this, and yet Danny had had almost no experiences of meaningful contact with children his own age. It felt as if Danny had been diagnosed with a virulent and pernicious cancer, and then been told off for feeling unwell. These contradictions affected his sense of being. His actions were treated as a matter of process and not praxis; however, he was then criticized for these as though they were recognized actions over which he was in complete and total control.

When I first met Danny it was in his class at school, and, although he seemed untroubled by my presence, I immediately noticed he had a large bruise above his left eye. His teacher informed me this had been sustained from banging his head against a drawer when he had become distressed. He was sitting alone in the corner of the room playing with a box of stickle bricks while the rest of his class were sitting attentively focused on the teacher at the front of the room. I explained the reason for our meeting, and he engaged freely, informing me he would be happy to attend a session with me the following week. Although he spoke confidently and articulately, he chose to communicate through two different characters he had created, and represented them using his hands as though they were puppets. He named them "Snakie" and "Parrot". The snake was described as naughty, and at different times he took weapons from Danny's pocket to hit either himself or the parrot.

Over the next few sessions, Danny was always happy to attend, although when I came to collect him from class he was always sitting on the fringe, having removed himself from the rest of his classmates. On the third session, he came in confidently and began to describe how he used to like dinosaurs very much, but didn't now, having been scared by one he saw in a museum. He told me how he had seen a dinosaur moving and that it had eaten another one: his father, he later added, had to take him home and comfort him. He then began a long monologue about dinosaurs, discussing how they lived and how they originally had evolved out of the sea. He drew pictures of dinosaurs, separating them out into two categories, the carnivores, who were the "baddies", and those which lived in a "land of myths", the "leaf eaters". Throughout the narrative, he spoke almost continuously, leaving little space for response. He then played with some toy farm animals in the room, again separating them into two groups, suggesting that if they were mixed together they might "lose their own kind", although he added that certain babies were allowed to "go together". He explained how God made babies and gave them to your parents to look after, except one time when the baby ran away. He went on to describe an occasion on which he had run away and hidden in a bush until his mother grabbed him and had to speak to the police. He spoke a little about the sheep and the sheepdog that rounded them up. He ended his play by telling me he once knew someone who clipped the wings of a bird to stop it flying. This happened because the bird was naughty and a "pain in the arse".

The next session, when I came to collect Danny from class, he addressed me straight away with his hand shaped like the puppet snake. Snakie was causing trouble. He had recently been in a fight with another child in which he had been particularly aggressive and he was very unremorseful. He continued to speak through the Snakie character, explaining how he did not like to be held or picked up, and would hit out at others in response. Children, he whispered, can be really dangerous, and if the snake becomes really angry, he, too, will grow out of control. From an existential position, we can see aspects of Danny in all characters of the narrative, both the scared snake, lashing out in fear, and the children who intimidate it. His mother, he continued, used a wrist strap on him, but this made him very angry. He explained that a restraint would not be able to hold Snakie and would just make him angry. Danny did say he had once bought a cage that was also unable to hold Snakie. He had tried to sell him or give him away, but he would always bite any prospective buyers and ". . . he's a big pain in the arse". At the end of the session, he put the snake away in his pocket, but it was able to dig a hole and escape out of the room.

Several sessions later, he spoke again about birds which had their wings clipped to prevent them from flying. He informed me it was cruel to stop them flying. When they tried to flap their wings, the air would go through them and they could not take off. He spoke about small animals and small children, describing them as freedom fighters, telling me they had to fight for themselves and not for other people. This led on to conversation about a hypothetical war between children and adults: "the grown-ups wouldn't stand a chance". When questioned about our relationship, Danny said he would not hurt me, but if he was in charge of the school and of our sessions they would all work better. He was adamant that he could "outsmart me . . . at fighting".

It seemed apparent that the contradictions in the way adults around Danny related to him were magnified in his own self-perception. The way in which he was able to understand his own being was caught in contradictory ideas of power and control. On the one hand, he was constrained by his parents' overbearing boundaries, the constraints of his ADHD diagnosis, or the negative rejection he had received from his nursery and infant schools. On the other hand, his actions had become extremely powerful, disproportionately influencing his parents life, forcing his mother to give up work, move him from one school to another, and enabling him to govern so much of his own time in class. The isolation thrust upon him from the way his behaviour had been managed meant he had little opportunity to regulate his own sense of identity in relation to others in an everyday manner.

During one session, Danny came into the room and asked to paint. He sat away from the paints and brushes, however, and began to paint instead on the page, using only water. He drew a large rectangle on one side of the page and on top of it something that looked like a television aerial. He was clearly interested in the water going through the paper and he repeatedly lifted it to look underneath and feel the texture of the page. When he finally began to use the paint, it was to draw a white outline over the area he had already marked out. He then painted white bars across it, before asking me to guess what it was. He soon revealed that it was a "Robot Cyber-Shrinker", able to shrink things and turn them into robots. He added an additional black coloured box in the corner of the page, describing this as the "Control Satellite" sending out orders. When I tried to explore this further with Danny, he did not respond explicitly to my questions, choosing instead to focus on mixing the coloured paint. He mixed all the colours together in a steady and deliberate manner, concentrating with great intensity. During this period of the session he spoke very little, until I reminded him it was nearly the end of our session. He then continued to paint, marking out a large dark rectangle around the control satellite, encircling it and containing it. In the corner of this perimeter box, he depicted a bright eye in red and yellow paint looking out over the satellite, as well as his robot machine. Just before we left the session Danny experimented by pouring all the remaining colours into a mixing pot. He asked if he could leave this mixture in the room and return to it next week, which we did.

Progress in my work with Danny was slow and sessions were often repetitive. Despite the way he had been rejected through much of his education, he was, however, still an incredibly articulate and imaginative child.

The metaphorical image Danny viewed of himself in the mirror was a shattered and disordered one. His "sense of reality" had become torn apart to such an extent that he understood himself as both tormentor and tormented. It appeared to me that he had taken seriously what he had been taught previously by his previous school and his family. As he became more aware of the double standards with which he was both controlled and chastised, he was increasingly bewildered. The situation he found himself in was untenable: compelled to engage with other children, but also restricted from doing so; told on the one hand his behaviour should be less impulsive and more controlled, and on the other that he was so easily influenced it would not even be appropriate for him to watch television. To create and reflect on new experiences in our sessions was vital. The progress we made together was not simply from understanding the contradictions in his world-view, but also in providing a new reliable and consistent relationship. All these new experiences provided opportunity for us to reflect and nurture a new way of relating. The sessions I spent reviewing with Danny's parents also emerged as crucial opportunities for them to reflect on their role in maintaining these messages of contradiction.

By the time I met with his parents at the end of our work together in order to review his progress, the transformation he had undergone was great. Both parents were very pleased with how he had become more settled in school over the previous six months. They spoke extensively about his home–school diary, which was now filled with positive comments on a daily basis. His father, in particular, described how he felt Danny had "grown up" and, importantly, he was able to reflect on his own role in allowing this to happen. When we further explored what this meant for him, he was able to provide examples of Danny taking more responsibility at home, being allowed to make choices for himself. They had removed a block from their television, allowing him potential access to all the channels, and expressed how they felt confident to take him out to restaurants. When discussing the increased empathy he was showing towards his peers, they added he had become close to one particular child in his class, whom he now called a friend. As well as feeling close to one of his classmates, there was also a child whom he regularly came into conflict with. Both these relationships illustrated a stark contrast to Danny six months before, when he struggled to relate to any of the children in his school, choosing only to address adults or remove himself from any social situation. His parents described each of our review meetings as challenging but productive. They said they had spent a long time considering how much they were constraining Danny, and while this had not enabled them to change every aspect of how they related to him, it had allowed them to make huge strides towards allowing him greater freedom and responsibility.

Cui bono?

It is common, in my experience, for all family members to have a strong investment in the patterns of different relationships and dynamics that have been allowed to develop. The therapist must, effectively, ask what the parents and other family members stand to gain by certain behaviours continuing. However painful and upsetting it may be for a parent to see their child suffer with the same high levels of anxiety they experienced as a child, it may also enable them to relate to their child with greater understanding. This, in turn, may also bring with it other outcomes, such as maintaining a level of professional input into the family, creating or maintaining an identity for the family unit as victims or as being fragile, and so on. It may offer the parents an outlet on to which they can direct many of the frustrations they feel in their own relationships, without needing to take the difficult step of confronting these issues or each other.

I was once asked to accompany a health visitor to a meeting with an anxious mother of a four-year-old child just about to start school. The mother described to me her son's behaviour as becoming so uncontrollably violent that she was unable to leave him for just a moment. She even had to give up driving recently, as it had become necessary for her to sit alongside him on the back seat of the car. If ever away from him for just a brief moment, she would become extremely anxious that something may happen. As we spoke, she went on to explain to me how she had never been able to express herself throughout her childhood, due to the strict nature of her upbringing, and this had had a severe impact on her ability to take risks (both physically and emotionally). It seemed that, however demanding and exhausting her son's behaviour had become, it also met a need in her, and was no doubt influenced by her own world-view and highly anxious and controlling identity.

It is important for a therapist working with children to reflect on how, and, indeed, why, a family may complain about the so-called symptoms of their child's given "pathology" without actually acknowledging the function it performs within the family structure. The parents will, no doubt, experience genuine frustration at times towards seemingly eccentric or unpredictable behaviour. None the less, they may simultaneously perpetuate the circumstances and patterns of expectation that act to bring about these deeds they claim to dislike.

*Care (*Sorge*)*

The German term *sorge* was used by Heidegger to denote our existential relationship to the world. We never exist in isolation; we are never alone and always exist in relation to our 'Being-in-the-world'. *Sorge* is often translated as meaning "care", in this case, our care for the world. This does not mean we are ecologically minded or altruistic to all people we meet, but instead are always concerned about our world. Cohn (2002) prefers his own translation of "involvement", adding that, as living beings, we have "involvement with those who are with us". It is also useful to consider how Heidegger uses the word *world* to denote not just the physical, planetary sphere on which we live, but also a world of people: a world of other living people, with cultures, ideas, and history into which we are thrown without choice. Each child is born into the world with no say regarding whether he or she would choose to be there. They are, essentially, thrown into existence. To clarify, we have shown that there is never a singular "subject" existing in isolation without a world or without others. We are always involved with the world and always, "thus find phenomenally that *knowing is a kind of Being which belongs to Being-in-the-world*" (Heidegger, 2000, p. 88). As existing beings, we are concerned with our own sense of Being and fascinated by the world with which we are concerned.

Hand in hand with our "falling" into being-in-the-world is an inevitable pull towards inauthenticity. "Falling Being-in-the-world is not only tempting and tranquillizing; it is at the same time *alienating*" (*ibid.*, p. 222). Here, Heidegger refers to the way we are all alienated, for the most part, from an understanding of ourselves, something we only really encounter in true ontological states (such as anxiety). It is through a state of genuine anxiety that we may become aware of ourselves, but this is not a functional, everyday state, which allows us to go about our daily lives. In a state of anxiety, we are unable to drive to work, eat our breakfast, and so on. In this state, we are turned from our everyday "lostness" in the general mass of society and are aware of our own existence in a different manner. However, as we are already aware, this authentic awareness, although it may be disclosive and an opportunity for growth and developing greater self-understanding, is not a pleasant experience and does not allow us to function.

This state is a distinct contrast to our everyday lives, in which we are unaware of our being, and also, essentially, unaware of our choices. Throughout much of our everyday life, we are all making choices constantly. For example, about where to sit, what to eat, where to move, what I should pick up, and so on. The likelihood of falling into what Sartre described as the concept of "Bad Faith" arrives when we turn away from the freedom granted to us by our falling into the world, with the choices that inevitably accompany this, and our concern (or, precisely, our involvement) for it. "I fall into bad faith if I take one or both of the two dishonest positions about reality: If I pretend either to be free in a world without facts or to be a fact in a world without freedom" (Cannon, 1991, p. 46).

Understanding, then, is torn away from a state of authenticity and into the "they", and man is, essentially, fallen. Heidegger describes this state as being lost in the "they" (*das man*). Within a therapeutic session, it would not be appropriate or, indeed, deliberately possible to bring about a state of true authenticity in a child, but the therapist is able to encourage reflection on the choices made.

Particularly within educational settings, children are reminded of their choices. When a child has become frustrated and angry, they may be encouraged to make the right choice or the wrong choice, a good choice or a bad choice. This is an encouraging progression within educational thinking about managing challenging behaviour, but if this process is to be employed therapeutically, it must arrive without moral judgement. This form of engaging children is used in essence as direction and, although certainly more welcome than draconian measures of discipline left over from Victorian notions of childhood, it is not truly encouraging self-reflection or greater self-awareness. The role of the school or educational institution in this case is to socialize the child, in order to fit in with the particular regulations and limits of acceptable expression (Szasz, 1973). If this type of engagement is to be truly therapeutic for a child, it must not provide parameters that can act to take away the authenticity of a unique experience. I am not, of course, suggesting that children should be allowed to break out into a wild rage in the classroom to the danger of themselves and their peers in order to gain increased self-awareness. This does, however, raise questions about the context in which therapeutic interventions take place: how containing they are, how safe they are (both physically and emotionally), and the scope to which emotional experience could be managed. All these questions are crucially important, not only to the school and family, but equally to the therapist, who must, of course, consider their own limitations.

Solicitude (Fursorge)

Care and concern relate to the fundamental "being-with" aspect of our existence. As established in the tradition of existential thought, we, as living and existing non-pluralistic individuals, always exist in relation to other people. We always have a concern of, or for, others, even if this is in a way of passing each other by without mattering to one another. Heidegger's writing tells us also that the way in which we care for the world is through "solicitude" (*Fursorge*). His use of the word solicitude is related to "care" (*sorge*), and he describes it as, "the concern of one Dasein for another Dasein". This notion of solicitude takes two distinct forms, one of "leaping in" (*Einspringen*) and one of "leaping ahead" (*Vorspringen*).

With the "leaping in" type of solicitude, we are taking away the care for other individuals in order to retain it as something of our own, or to give it back, returning it as something to be "got rid of". With the "leaping ahead" level of solicitude, we are not taking away care, but creating an awareness in which an authenticity, related to the existential givens of our being, is given back to the other. Within many therapeutic sessions there may be periods of silence, most notably when a child is enacting a narrative or illustrating an experience. These circumstances could also be punctuated, however, by great tension. A child may, for example, have been encouraged to attend a session against his initial instincts, and, upon entering the session, already be in a state of anger or frustration. Here, the therapist is faced with many choices, and it would certainly be unwise to advocate forcing children to attend a session under any circumstances. There may, however, be some ambivalence for the child; they did not want to come, but, once in the room, new opportunities have arisen to relate to their therapist or express themselves in a new experience. The temptation for the therapist may be to leap in and try to take away the tension that has arisen, perhaps by reassuring the child that they do not need to attend, as they had previously been told. There is also an opportunity for the therapist and child to see their relationship in a new light and to explore what was different between this session and any other. In order for this to occur, the experience of the tension is a valuable foundation on which to base further exploration. Here, the therapist may be leaping ahead. The tendency for the first way of engaging, in which the therapist "leaps in" will be for a dependency to build up, as the child relies upon the therapist to ease or remove the difficult experience by presenting a solution. This does not happen if the therapist enables the child to find a way to meet his or her own difficulties. This is, fundamentally, not providing answers or clear direction, but a process of facilitation. The relevance of this distinction for practising psychotherapy is certainly worth considering, and this is particularly salient in work with children.

The kind of solicitude that leaps in and takes away "care" is, to a large extent, determinative for being with one another, and alludes, for the most part, to our concern with the world around us and all it contains. By contrast, however, there is also the possibility of the second kind of solicitude, which, as we have demonstrated, does not so much leap in for the child as leap ahead of them into their possibility, not in order to take away care, but rather to give it back to them, "authentically as such for the first time" (Heidegger, 2000, p. 159). The possibility for the "leaping ahead" aspect of solicitude is also present in family relationships. This solicitude relates to the authentic care of parents for their children, that is to say, to their existence and not something tangible with which they are concerned. This solicitude allows children to become open to seeing themselves and their possibility.

Again, for parents, it is easy to misunderstand the balance that must clearly be struck in providing sufficient consistency and safety to enable a child to develop a strong and secure sense of their own being and who they are. The opportunity to become aware of the possibilities inherent in the leaping ahead of solicitude does not mean a child should be abandoned to experience the challenges of life alone. By contrast, it actually acknowledges the true humanity of a child in a unique and new situation. It is only upon reflection that it may be possible to consider and acknowledge to ourselves how often we do not really encounter others around us as separate individuals existing in the same way as us. All too often, they are experienced as a tool or component of a task, enabling us to complete the action we are engaged in. Someone selling a ticket to a football match simply becomes a stage in the process of entering the stadium. A distressed child often may become simply an object to tame in order to restore a calm environment. If the child is to truly be recognized as a living being we must not remove their responsibility.

Ollie

The context in which children arrive at their first session reveals their world-view: their experiences of living, their Being-in-the-world. Ollie, an eight-year-old boy, was initially referred by his school, where the staff recently had been struggling to manage his behaviour in class. When they referred him for therapy, he was on the point of exclusion, and it was clear that the anxiety levels among the staff who taught him were already high. They cited how he often became aggressive when annoyed, and had developed a tendency to storm out of the classroom when being disciplined by teachers or confronted by other adults with the repercussions of his actions.

Ollie's class teacher had developed strong feelings, becoming quite harassed and stressed by his consistent displays of disobedience and her experiences of being undermined by him, in front of her class. While the issues were clearly related to the context of his outbursts, I agreed to offer therapeutic sessions to Ollie if they were able to take place in school.

As with all primary care community referrals of this nature, after discussing the circumstances with the referrer, my initial interview was with Ollie's parents. By the time of our first appointment, his parents were aware of the reasons for our meeting and the potential for therapeutic work to be offered to Ollie. Typically, however, I began by restating the nature of our meeting, to encourage greater reflection and some consideration of both of their personal responsibilities in encouraging their son to engage in this potentially new relationship. Although the choice to attend and really, truly engage always lies with the child themselves, the intrinsic nature of a family, viewed metaphorically as an organism in its own right, means that every member bears some responsibility at the outset of such a journey. As I began to explain who I was, my professional role, and the services I could hope to offer, both of Ollie's parents became increasingly nervous and hesitant. His father was first to say that "This all seems a bit much . . . I'm not sure if any of this is really necessary."

They discussed the anxieties they saw in Ollie, his nervousness in front of his peers, and the way he would remove himself from public gaze when he became distraught. His mother interjected,

"He's such a timid, sensitive boy . . . I guess he's just like me really, I can't stand being different, standing up in front of people . . . in fact, I particularly remember our wedding day; it was one of the hardest days of my life, and yet I know it shouldn't have been like that." As they continued to describe their experiences and each member's role within the family, they explained how they had already spoken to Ollie at some length about the potential benefits of attending sessions. He had been reluctant for anyone in school to know of this and absolutely forbade his parents to let him be taken out of lessons to attend sessions: the same lessons he left very conspicuously himself on a regular basis.

When Ollie finally came for his first session, he had agreed to attend at the end of the day, after all his classmates had left, and initially he had asked for his mother to accompany him. When they first arrived, Ollie was extremely nervous and hid behind his mother's body, like an anxious toddler hiding from the world. He sat down but spoke very little. Almost every question I asked was filtered through Ollie's mother before he felt able to respond. She offered him forced choice alternatives with which to respond to me and little space was left open for a true disclosure of how Ollie felt. "How do you feel about coming here today?"

"Tell Chris what you said to me this morning on the way to school."

"What have you been doing today?"

"Do you want to tell him about football or what happened this afternoon?"

On our second meeting, Ollie again arrived with his mother, and began by pointing out to me that he had not been naughty in school at all recently. After reviewing the previous session, he agreed for his mother to step out of the session, but was insistent she waited close by on the school premises. Ollie went on to discuss his experiences playing football. In particular, he described recently being awarded a prize at an end of season ceremony by a team he played for. He added that he had already received more than twenty awards from the different teams he played for. He spoke about how uncomfortable he felt collecting any award in front of a crowd and how self-conscious he felt when being watched. When we drew up a contract together for our sessions, it was noticeable how Ollie focused on the perceptions of others and a sense of fairness. "I think we should have no name calling . . . and no talking behind each other's backs." In future sessions, he contrasted his experiences of being watched while playing football and being awarded prizes after. Even when many people watched him play, he informed me he did not feel at all nervous.

As the sessions continued he seemed to grow in confidence, but there was always a brief dialogue at the start or end of the session enquiring as to the exact time we would finish, start, and whether he should remind his parents where to collect him from. This went on for the first twelve sessions. During the tenth session, he constructed a narrative around a worried-looking face he drew on a large sheet of paper. He told me that this person had lost (as in a game of football), but then changed this to the person being lost in the woods without their parents. In the distance, he continued, he could hear the car of a "stranger" approaching. This character then became a "robber in the shadows" and it was soon apparent that the fear and worry he expressed was of the unknown. It was not a fear of the character he had created, but of the potential; not of what happened, but of what might have played out. He added detail to the story, explaining how this person could not be seen and he could not tell who it was.

Ollie also told me how nervous he was about delivering a short line in a recent school assembly. He described shaking all over his body, but that no one else was nervous or worried. He identified one girl in particular as confident, "because she's clever". Of apparently little significance to him was that the rest of the school was unaware of his shaking. "I don't think anyone could tell," he informed me.

A few sessions later, Ollie again created a narrative in which a boy returned from school and was chased home by a witch. The boy ended up hiding in a cupboard from the witch, who had threatened to transform him into a different creature, "perhaps a flying fish, able to fly away". Ollie was able to describe the emotions and experiences of the boy's many fears and how he later became more empowered, eventually sneaking up on the witch in order to defend himself. Ollie drew the boy, having closed himself in the cupboard, trying to hide as quietly as possible but, at the same time, knowing he could be heard by the witch. The witch was depicted in the corner of the page climbing in the window cackling to herself,

"Ha, ha, I've heard him." The narrative soon ended in a bloody and violent manner, with the boy stabbing the witch and running away before he could see if she had died.

Only after Ollie was able to experience and later confront his own difficult emotions was there the possibility for him to transparently see himself. It was important to attend to the ability for a young child like Ollie to transcend his family circumstances. The anxiety felt so overwhelmingly by his mother was gifted to Ollie through the way she related to him on a daily basis. His talent in football meant that he was frequently in the public eye and performing in front of large crowds, even at the age of just eight. The fear he experienced alongside this was demonstrated to me through his pictures, depicting ghosts and the figure of the witch emerging from the woods and chasing the boy with a knife. A pattern had developed within the family for Ollie to noticeably display his anxiety, and for his mother subsequently to oblige in taking it away. Her care for him became too great, and his autonomy was not recognized or acknowledged. In school, it was possible to see how Ollie fled when confronted by his fears as he pre-empted the possibilities inherent in his own anxiety. In many ways, his teacher, too, fed into these reactions through her worrying about his potential defiance. This was not addressed directly in school, and perhaps the option of being able to refer Ollie to a professional from outside the school community enabled her to avoid the challenge of confronting the tension in the class.

When Ollie was allowed to experience these anxieties and authentically see himself, this facilitated him in taking greater responsibility. This relied on not being drawn, as the therapist, into feeling anxious for Ollie and needing to rescue him, jumping in and taking away his self-care. Thus, through a new relationship, he became able to develop greater autonomy and not be dominated by his fears or his family.

CHAPTER SEVEN

Existential psychotherapy and psychoanalysis

> "Tell me how you are searching and I will tell you what you are searching for"
>
> (Wittgenstein, 1980, p. 3)

Central to the practice of psychoanalytic psychotherapy is an initial belief in the assumption that internal processes are at play with influences from the external world in shaping our emotional states and their development. The way in which these internal processes interact with their external counterparts, however, is something of a long-running debate within the psychoanalytic community (although, modern trends appear to lean more towards the importance of the intersubjective relationship). It has even been suggested that such divisions of internal and external influences are ambiguous or confusing unless one is viewed as directly influencing the other (Gill, 1994). Undoubtedly, these modern shifts towards further acknowledging the influence of the relationship as crucial to the psychotherapeutic process bring psychoanalysis closer to the ideas of existential therapies. Despite this movement, significant differences do still exist. Throughout this book, many points of convergence and divergence between existential and other (perhaps more traditional) psychotherapies practised with children have been highlighted. In order to provide greater clarification, however, this chapter aims to underline a more direct comparison of some of the core principles of practising existential or psychoanalytic-based psychotherapies with children.

There are certainly similarities to be found in the philosophies of both approaches, and it is possible to say that the early case studies, from which Freud derived and then presented many of his initial theories, emerge from the rich Germanic tradition of the existential novella. Within these narratives, the reader can see the crises of identity into which his patients are thrown, and the strong influence of a social and family dynamic on their own fundamental ontology.

Key to understanding the essential differences between existential and analytic approaches, however, is a willingness to closely examine and draw into question the rigidity of two primary splits: between body and mind, and a subject and their world. Also of value in initiating debate around a potential role for existential practice with children is to further consider an existential understanding of childhood development, choice, and its opposition to reductive interpretation.

Although psychoanalytic theories and practices have evolved significantly since the ideas of Freud, he still remains a benchmark for comparison within the field. Other theories are frequently described by means of their divergence from Freudian thought. In many ways, his ideas and vocabulary have infiltrated our daily lives, and terms such as "resistance", "defensive behaviour", and even "the unconscious" itself are now in common use and taken for granted. Freudian concepts are often employed as a starting point for subsequent psychotherapeutic theory, in the same way that water can be perceived as neutral in taste. From this central, neutral position, a drink could be described as salty, sweet, sour, or acidic. However, like the ideas of Freud, this neutral starting point rests on many initial assumptions, which are frequently unacknowledged. In effect, water has a taste, but one which has become so much a part of our everyday lives that it is forgotten and its qualities are almost indescribable.

Dualism

The seventeenth-century French philosopher, René Descartes, sought to radically overhaul the philosophical tradition in which he found himself by returning to a tradition of questioning all aspects of life. In questioning the world around him, he began to draw conclusions about the starting position from which his thoughts evolved. He concluded that, since he was able to conceive such sceptical and questioning thoughts to begin with, these thoughts he was generating must have come from something—a self, a subject, an "I".

> But I have convinced myself that there is absolutely nothing in the world, no sky, no earth, no minds, no bodies. Does it follow then that I too do not exist? No: if I convinced myself of something then I certainly existed . . . So after considering everything very thoroughly, I must finally conclude that this proposition, I am, I exist, is necessarily true whenever it is put forward by me or conceived in my mind. [Descartes, 1966, p. 64]

In the assertion *cogito ergo sum* (I think therefore I am), Descartes firmly places the personal preposition "I" as the starting point for any subsequent conclusions. Through his process of questioning and enquiry, he even questions the existence of the world: "How do you know that a world exists? After all, your belief that there is an external world is merely based on your sensations" (Descartes, 1993). Here, the existential philosophy of Heidegger makes a sharp and radical contrast. He points out that Descartes position of questioning the world relies already upon some knowledge of what a world is. Essentially, knowing is a form of our existence, founded upon our Being-in-the-world. In other words, our very existence in the world precedes any subsequent notions of knowledge. Prior to questioning the existence of the world, Descartes himself must already *exist*, and do so with all the existential "givens" which affect us all, including always being in the context of a world.

These ideas of Descartes formed the foundations of logical philosophy and, indeed, are a cornerstone of modern psychology and natural sciences. His beliefs also have significant implications for how we discuss our "selves" and the world. A temptation, to which much early psychoanalytic thought succumbed, was to focus excessively, I believe, on the unique and singular experiences of the individual, and a vocabulary to describe relationships between *individual people* has predominated. Here, the intersubjective processes are lost, and a true representation of a shared, collective experience becomes more distant.

The observations John Bowlby carried out of mothers and their infants at the London Child Guidance Clinic highlighted the importance of relationship on a child's development. In many ways, his ideas complemented the work of Donald Winnicott, adding weight to the growing contradictions at the time of such a strong reliance (in traditional psychoanalysis) on internal and intrapsychic drives as influences on childhood development. Importantly, Bowlby also draws attention (1988) to the fact that it is *perceptions* of the behaviour of mother and child interactions in which he is interested. Frequently, throughout his later writing, we can see that the information he records is described as "observations" and also occur in "certain sorts of defined situations". Here, like the existential therapist, there is an acknowledgement being made of the therapist or psychologist as a distinct part of the process, as well as the context they are in. In short, his theory becomes based upon observable experiences and not on so-called facts or indisputable internal processes. He does not start by prising the individual infant away from their world, of which the researching psychologist is also a part.

Body and mind

Not only did Descartes suggest a split of the individual as a pluralistic entity distinguishable from its world, but also a division of body and mind. This distinction appears less pronounced in modern psychology and psychoanalytic theory than it perhaps once was, but is again a split that can still be seen existing largely unchallenged in western thought. Within contemporary neuroscience, ever greater strides have been made in identifying the links between a child's physical environment and its influences on the corporeal body, most notably around the development of significantly altered or impaired neural pathways in the brains of children who have been deprived of appropriate stimulation and affection.

Along with an acknowledged division of body and mind, however, comes the challenge of linking psychological, emotional, and mental experiences to the observable activity of the brain. The activation of a specific neural pathway may be an integral component to the actual experience of an emotion, but one is not the other. Descartes speculatively identified the pineal gland as the central point of conjunction for the body and mind, and, although neurological sciences have advanced incomparably since his time, the division still persists. How are our felt experiences relayed to our minds, and how is it that powerful emotions, such as heartache and sorrow, can be experienced so physically within our bodies? Broadly speaking, existential psychotherapy and philosophy does not concern itself with this challenging dilemma, by starting from a position of what we observe and understand phenomenologically. As therapists, we are never presented with a body-less mind or a mind-less body. In front of us is simply a child. Throughout the life of each child they will only be perceived as a whole: "in fact whatever happens to us, whatever we do, involves both aspects of our Being, the physical and the non-physical, and can be perceived as such" (Cohn, 2002, p. 106).

Although existential psychotherapy does not concern itself with identifying such distinctions, the language of separating so-called "mental" process from the physical body continue to be widespread. Even the term *psychotherapy* represents the pervasiveness of this established vocabulary and could be looked upon as a somewhat misleading term by suggesting we should be occupied with a therapy of the "psyche". If I asked a child to draw an image of their "psyche", or mind, they may either depict a brain, the control centre for many of the body's functions, or they may choose to draw an image from their experiences, that is to say, what they are thinking about. This illustrates how our being is always embodied (through the image of the brain), or related to the world of our concern (through an image of a memory). The role of the existential psychotherapist is not to treat, understand, or even attend to the mind or psyche of a child, but to work with the whole child. This, in turn, can only take place in a relationship, and so, if we are to be honest about the real nature of such an endeavour, we must start by recognizing the relationship itself and not its individual components.

Reductive interpretation

The process of interpretation is effectively a reductive one, unless it can be offered from a position of uncertainty. By, for example, identifying to a child a toy figure as representative of a father, it is, by definition, excluding other possibilities: therefore, it loses the possibility of being a brother, son, cousin, monster, hero, and so on. Only if such interpretations can be posited as questions are they broadening. Existential psychotherapy aims to understand a child in a specific relationship at a specific time and place. From an opening position of acknowledging uniqueness of any given relationship, the therapist must abandon any preconceived theories and means for interpretative analysis. If the therapist approaches a session with a set view of restricted categories into which the presentation of the child could be placed, then they cannot be truly open and circumspect to a new experience. Although psychoanalysis is itself a broad church with a vast spectrum of ideas, it is, in essence, a theoretical framework from which to understand an encounter.

A child's choice to use a certain toy within their play can be given a specific meaning, which could be speculated upon, eventually being reduced to a "truer" symbolic reality. The burying of a toy figure in a sand tray during a session could be seen by the therapist as a symbol of repression or defensiveness. Viewed existentially, the same act should be understood by the therapist as unique to that situation and not representative of a symbolic or unconscious communication. The phenomena is primarily noticed and observed for what it is. The therapist may enquire about the experience of the act itself or of the toy; they may reflect on what a process of burying may potentially mean for the child, but at the core of the interaction must remain openness. If the child's understanding of an action or play activity radically contrasts with that of the therapist, then this contradiction could be acknowledged and provide a fertile ground for dialogue. Core to this process, however, is the opening up of possibility.

Freudian psychoanalysis

Heidegger allegedly remarked to Medard Boss in his *Zollikon Seminars* that a potential understanding of the word "analysis" could be derived from one of its connotations in the original Greek language, "to loosen, for instance, to release a chained person from his chains, to liberate someone from captivity" (Heidegger, 2001, p. 312).

Freud often seemed to allude to a human capacity for freedom in choice and the possibility of the disclosure of truth. However, he was also dedicated to what Heidegger rather damningly referred to as the "dictatorship" of science. His dependence on Cartesian dualism and the dichotomy of a subject–object existence led him towards assuming the existence of an unknown internal power controlling our external physicality. Heidegger saw Freud's "metapsychology" as a combination of the application of Kantian objectivity and the natural sciences (*ibid.*, p. 208). He indicated that Freud postulated our phenomena were based on causal connections, which are not present in the conscious and must be effected in an "unconscious".

> The postulate is the complete explanation of psychical life whereby explanation [Erklaren] and understanding [Verstehen] are identified. This postulate is not derived from the psychical phenomena themselves but is a postulate of modern natural science. [*ibid.*]

What seems to be absent is a salient regard for the experience of the relationship that occurs between two individuals, child and therapist, and, hence, the responsibility of choice.

Man is a free thinking and self-aware being. This distinguishes us from animals, whose functioning is determined by their instinctual forces. They find their behaviour controlled by their desires and drive to survive. These drives have been predetermined by inherited neurological structures. Through the processes of evolution, we can see how an animal is adapted and suited to evolve to its environment, optimally equipping itself through genetic adaptation to meet its conditions. Nature can, of course, provide threats to the life of an individual plant or animal, but its goal and inherent drives still dictate much of its activity. A honeybee, for example, may encounter certain predators, but its disposition will still be to gather nectar and, in so doing, pollinate flowers. Man, however, is different. We have an awareness of ourselves and our being, and, hence, of the limitations and givens with which we exist. We cannot choose to be born, and we cannot escape our own mortality. We always exist in relation to others and the world. Between these existential givens there is no inherited defining mission justifying our existence. As Fromm writes,

> Man's life cannot "be lived" by repeating the pattern of his species; he must live . . . Man is the only animal who finds his own existence a problem which he has to solve and from which he cannot escape. [Fromm, 1976, p. 24]

This struggle is born out of the meaninglessness of life. As can be seen in the work of Sartre, "existence precedes essence": we are born without direct purpose, unlike the purpose of the honeybee, which maintains a place in tune with nature. Human instincts, of course, do inevitably exist, but in a very different capacity. In being alive, most people are influenced by a desire to continue to survive, and, in doing so, feel compelled to eat, drink, and have sex. However, these human compulsions also create choices, making them different to instinctual drives. A person who regularly drinks excessive amounts of alcohol may feel compelled to drink more at any given time; further alcohol in their bloodstream may even be a physical requirement of their body in order to prevent the onset of a seizure. However, they may also later show regret or remorse at the repercussions of their excessive alcohol consumption. What they are alluding to here is an element of choice. The act itself may take place without reflection, but if it is accompanied by guilt or remorse, this can only occur if the person is aware of some level of freedom to have made an alternative choice.

Man is the only being who appears to demonstrate this type of self-awareness. This allows a context for dissatisfaction and unrest, it allows us to experience boredom, it allows us to feel disillusioned at times, and it even creates the possibility for self-destruction. When an infant is born into the world it is vulnerable and helpless, even more so than when in the womb from which it came. If an infant is to develop from the point of birth, an act over which it exercises no control, to becoming a human being, it must develop a concern for the world and its own existence. It must learn to cope with the world in order to survive. This takes place through a process of increased self-perception brought about only through relating with others.

Intersubjectivity

A child is not born as a singular creation existing in isolation. There is, undeniably, always a child and a mother, if only for a few brief moments. There is never just a child alone. The child's world may appear cold, barren, and isolated compared to the womb it has just left, but each child's existence is inherently intersubjective. From an existential perspective, the development a child must go through to reach adulthood is not a linear progression of becoming a mature finished individual. In effect, the child already has a primordial experience of being with others, and it is a greater understanding of this that will grow and develop as the child moves towards being an adult.

The development of this understanding may be punctuated by significant events and stages, such as recognition of its own image or recognition of other people as something similar to itself (Merleau-Ponty, 1992). The challenge in these milestones for the developing child is not seeing its own image in a mirror and knowing it as an individual child, but the realization that the image he sees is his own image and, subsequently, what others see of him. In short, he is becoming increasingly aware of his place in the world.

The significance of this emerging understanding of a relational existence is great. It is our context and our relational world that provide us with a place in space and time. This guides our thoughts, our understanding, and, ultimately, how we experience the world. These levels of understanding contrast greatly with traditional psychoanalytic stages of development, primarily because they are not driven by such strong and deterministic instincts. We are fundamentally always "becoming", striving towards betterment and being ahead of ourselves. Human existence is essentially not comparable to the growth of an apple, reaching a decisive point of maturity at which it is at its ripest and sweetest. For the apple, after it has reached its maturity, begins to deteriorate and degrade, having passed its optimum. This is not the case for a child or adult at any point of maturity; there is no essential set goal at which a person could be said to be at their ultimate completion. In the psychoanalytic tradition, it is the periods of growth leading up to maturation that appear to affect the outcome of the final fruit.

Has the fruit progressed through the appropriate stages in the appropriate environment? A dysfunctional disruption during these predetermined stages affects the end product. As the fruit deprived of water and sunlight may become bitter and unpalatable, so, too, may the child who has been unable to pass through the gateways of psychosexual maturity without completion become bitter and unpalatable to themselves or the society in which they live.

Free will and choice

As a young infant develops, they are also confronted with the reality that even if they are able to realize their bodily cravings and compulsions, they will still experience all the emotional upheaval associated with the human condition. The struggles of creating meaning and direction in our life as a unique individual in space and time remain inescapable. In his own unique and poetic way, Nietzsche expresses the paradox that exists:

> The fatality of his nature cannot be disentangled from the fatality of all that which has been and will be. He is not the result of a special design, a will, a purpose; he is not the subject of an attempt to attain to an "ideal of man" or an "ideal of happiness" or an "ideal of morality"—it is absurd to want to hand over his nature to some purpose or other. [Nietzsche, 2004, p. 88]

Conversely, Freud believed that it was possible to uncover our most powerful drive, and that he had identified it in the libido. This led on to his theories of psychosexual drives influenced by the development of a child's psyche through progressive stages.

Freud's early thoughts on childhood were embodied by his theories of infantile psychosexual stages of development. These were structured in a progressive, chronological order, following the changes in significance of various erotogenic zones: "oral", "anal", and "phallic". These erotogenic zones enable us to obtain sensuous pleasure which may satisfy our primary composite of sexuality—in Freudian theory, the importance and consequence of "drives" (*Triebe*). Energy in our bodies is centred around these drives, and in their demand for pleasure, our body aims to discharge tension. As

Smith writes, "They have an aim, which is always the discharge of tension by some sexual act. The mode of discharge will depend upon the source of the desire" (1999, p. 56).

The source of the desire will be controlled or determined by the stage of development the child is at, and by certain external environmental influences, such as their mother, in her symbiotic role of nurturer and carer. If these drives are not met, then the bodily tension augmenting the drive will fail to be placated and will not be released. This release failure will result in the occurrence of "fixation" in a particular developmental stage, because of this bodily, physiological, mechanical deprivation.

Fixation can be thought of in theses terms as part of a patient's pathology, and from the catalyst of the psychosexual drives, the patient can be affected beyond their infancy. In Freud's own words, "if, in short, a perversion has the characteristics of exclusiveness and fixation—then we shall usually be justified in regarding it as a pathological symptom" (Freud, 1905d).

This failure to fulfil the desire of psychosexual drives is not the only way that fixation may occur, but, conversely, fixation may not be the only pathological symptom of a lack of drive success of potential, and, at a broader level, these may not be the only outcomes and possibilities of unbalance and conflict in the developmental stages.

A psyche?

From an existential position, the most powerful influence on our emotional and psychological development emerges from our inability to evade the givens of our existence. In the face of our existence, we are always confronted by choices and, consequently, existential guilt. Guilt, that is, for the choices we have not taken; in each context opportunities and limitations are always created and yet we will only ever be able to choose one singular option. Challenged in this way it is natural for us to flee, in a sense, towards illusions of structure and social hierarchy, positioning our lives as either healthy, emotionally stable and in control, or negative, mentally ill, or pathological.

In *Beyond Good and Evil*, Nietzsche wrote,

> A thought comes when "it" wants to and not when "I" want, thus it is a falsification to say: the subject "I" is the condition for the predicate "think". It thinks: but there is . . . no immediate certainty that this "it" is just that famous old "I". [Bettelheim, 1983, p. 61]

We can see here how easy it is to fall into the trap of believing that our own thought process, at a conscious level, determines all of our thoughts and actions. This may be something that we hope to be true, and perhaps allow ourselves to believe it is such, and not the inconsiderate reality. A relational mode of understanding that lies between our being-in-the-world and being-with-others is, as I have alluded to earlier, inauthentic, and, for the most part, "lost in the they". This is important to remind ourselves of for the purpose of explanation, for it is not necessary to denounce the relation of "I" to a "self", but it is important to question it. We are always relational, non-pluralistic in our lives, and, as an abstract proposition, "I" is not "self".

By contrast, Freud's historical emphasis was on pregenital, infantile development and posits sufficient significance, I believe, to abdicate the control of drives from our consciousness. When these drives operate beyond our conscious control, then they become compulsions. Compulsion is a word that, in many contexts, is interchangeable with the notion of what Freud frequently referred to as "instincts". These instincts are present, and perhaps at their most powerful stage of synthesis, during our early years. If this is true, then we must consider whether these early psychosexual instincts can determine whom, or indeed what, we become in later life.

Freud talked about "disturbances of this process of development" in the second of his *Three Essays on The Theory of Sexuality* (1905d), as an "active" component of the organization of instincts in "pathological cases". This creates a worrying thought about the absence of power over our adult choices, as well as those of a child. Are we, at this Freudian, critical period in our maturation, completely at the mercy of external influences upon an internal psyche to be stored and retained in some type of pre-programmed desire to realize our "instincts" and levels of satisfaction? I am prompted here by the thoughts of Tolstoy, who reminds us in the last lines of *War and Peace*, "It is necessary to renounce a freedom that does not exist and to recognise a dependence of which we are not personally conscious" (Tolstoy, 1982, p. 1443).

Bettelheim suggests that Freud may have referred to Nietzsche in his own thoughts on the definition of the abstract meaning of "I" in terms of the human "psyche". It seems to me somewhat contradictory of Freud to promote the "I" above the "it", yet perpetuate a stage theory for development. Jacobs writes an even more blunt explanation of Freud's theory of psychosexual development: that it depends on three main hypotheses. The first of these is the existence of personality types in mature adults, that second, these are related to the child's experiences resulting from particular ways of child rearing, and third, "that the mouth, anus and phallus are erotogenic zones in early childhood" (1992, p. 114). Here, the connection between the infantile development stages and human personality is defined in a direct way, and Jacobs goes on to discuss validation for Kleineian theories surrounding what Freudians called the "anal" and "oral" characters. Others, such as Erikson, have drawn attention to the role of characterization from early childhood, but have questioned Freud's outline of the pregenital stages as carrying so much importance. Erikson researched the importance of ego identity in adolescence, with reference to the foundations of the human, adult character, or what we have sometimes previously referred to as a kind of philosophical "I".

Choice as an existential

A frequently heavy reliance on technique and predetermined ways of communicating could be seen to inhibit genuine connection and dialogue. In essence, what appears to be absent is, in fact, *choice*: in existential practice, the individual child is influenced by their context and history in the way that it discloses their understanding and allows them to cope with the world around them, but there is also the opportunity for each child to transcend their family and context as a free thinking individual.

As discussed already throughout the book, choice confronts us in every moment of our lives as adults: what to wear in the morning, what to have for breakfast, how we choose to work, indeed, which word we choose to write. However, the choices that confront young children on a daily basis are less apparent and exist, we could say, more "covertly". Heidegger wrote about the nature of existence and its relationship with choice. He informs us that we have no choice about our being-in-the-world or our active character, and that our very existence is in some way defined by an unavoidability of having to *do* and be active, even if only through inaction.

We do not, in other words, have the option of not being-in-the-world and, therefore, of not choosing or acting in relation to the givens (Heidegger's *existentials*) of our existence. Heidegger illustrates, then, that our very existence is dictated by the choices that we have to face and the subsequent actions we then take in relation to them. We are thrown into existence, and within the boundaries and limitations of our world we have to make choices. Choice, in this existential sense, is always present with us. It is, therefore, always present with children in much the same way. The only differences we can draw attention to at this stage between the choices of adults and children are those dictated by the differences of their worlds.

Central within all perspectives of existential psychotherapy is the importance of an individual's desire and ability to try to transcend their circumstances. We are all thrown into existence without a choice or purpose, and scramble around to try to find some direction to cling on to. Core to an existential perspective of therapeutic work is a rejection of the determinism implicit within any developmental model of stages and milestones.

The determinism of objective truths in the process of psychotherapy appears to exclude the human capacity of free choice that Freud himself sometimes promoted. Freedom and choice are of paramount importance to the relationship of existential phenomenological psychotherapy, and any exclusion of these forces a reliance on facts. Freud has often been accused of trying to construct a science of the mind. As Heaton wrote,

> He believed that all mental activity is determined and that free association leads to a repressed wish that lies in the unconscious causing the associations to dry up; thus he could infer the cause of the block of the associations. [2000, p. 15]

The uncovering of these revelations would, thus, require an observer and interpreter, and this is the role of the analyst. If the analyst were to make accurate and appropriate interpretations to understand the causal relations to actions, he would, in turn, require a theory. The theory of "cause and effect" lies within the realms of science, and it is then no surprise that Freud sought his refuge there. What is concerning with a "science of the mind'" is the importance of knowledge as indubitable certainty. From certainty there lies little choice, and the therapeutic relationship becomes one of expert and novice. As Heidegger suggested,

> My thesis is that the unfolding essence of the human being is the understanding of being [Seinverstandnis]. I can experience the unfolding essence of the human being from the understanding of being. This experience becomes a hypothesis only at the moment when I set myself the task of apprehending and observing the human being in a particular [scientific] way. [2001, p. 208]

The promotion of a form of biological determinism in pregenital stages of psychosexual development, which Freud substantiated with evidence from his own subjective interpretations of the behaviour of adult neurotics, represents a distinct contrast to the practice of existential psychotherapy. Even by the criteria of a pseudoscience, these stages still grow from fundamental assumptions about the individual, objective nature of our existence in the world contrasted with instinctual drives inherent in the nature of the human species.

James

James was just seven years old when he was referred to a National Health Service (NHS) Child and Adolescent Mental Health service. The request for help had come from the special needs school, for moderate learning difficulties, which he attended. He lived with his twin, a twelve-year-old sister, and his father. James had spent his early formative years, along with his sisters, living some distance away from his current home with his mother, who suffered with long-term drug and alcohol issues, using both to uncontrolled excess. All the children had periodic but unreliable contact with their mother during school holidays and occasionally at weekends.

James had a diagnosis of an Autistic Spectrum Disorder (ASD) and quite limited verbal communication abilities. He would speak only in short sentences of two or three words, and it appeared as though the lexicon of words he chose from was quite small. His comprehensive vocabulary, however, appeared broader than his verbal one. Following a long legal dispute, the children had eventually come to live with their father with little preparation and planning. James had struggled in a mainstream school for six months before starting in a specialist education provision, and the new school had then also begun to face difficulties with his behaviour. He was often violent and aggressive in class, regularly punching, kicking, and biting other pupils and staff. At home, his father had given up his job in order to care for the children, but still found it difficult to manage.

Within class, James was described by his teacher as showing little or no empathy for his peers. He never played with the other children and never shared any toy or game he may have been using. He had a tendency to laugh and become excited at the sight of other children being told off. The rest of the time he would retreat under desks or to a corner of the classroom, from where it could take great time and effort for the teachers to encourage him out. When he was excited, or even just slightly nervous, James would harm himself by biting his own hand around the base of the thumb. When living with his mother and first assessed by social services, the scarring on his hand was so bad from this biting that it was thought to have been caused by cigarette burns.

His father explained to me how James frequently took the blame for any accidents and fights when living with his mother, as he was perceived by his sisters as the weaker child. Verbally, he was clearly unable to defend himself. James' father was evidently overwhelmed by caring for him, and, through his high levels of anxiety, had begun to imprison him more and more. He kept the doors and windows locked at home and had built a high fence encircling the house and garden. Although he undoubtedly cared greatly for James, it was also apparent there was a polarized split, with James again always seen as the "naughty" child and his twin sister as the "good" child (his older sister was forced into a more parental role).

During our early sessions together, James would spend much of his time colouring red over the eyes of the dolls in the room. He described this as blood. Sometimes, he would pretend to have cut his own finger and then proceed to cover it in red paint or pen. His behaviour was repetitive and he would regularly perform these acts almost as rituals near the start of each session. After about eight weeks, he chose to pretend to be cutting my finger, and this also soon became part of his routine. When I explained that it would hurt if my finger were really cut, James would become animated and laugh excitedly at my potential discomfort. I would encourage him to play ball games in the session at the start. To begin with, he evidently found it a challenge to play "with" me, and for me to really be included in the game. He was reluctant to take turns and was just as happy to throw the ball at me, rather than towards me. I continued with a focus on these types of simple games, taking turns, and endeavouring to build a relationship. We reflected on the emotional experiences in the sessions, particularly his laughing and arousal at my potential discomfort. After some time, James progressed to cleaning the figures whose eyes he had coloured, developing more of a caring and nurturing attitude. At the end of one session he asked if I could bring a plaster with me next time, and then a bandage, which he later used each week to repair the pretend wounds he had inflicted upon us both. As he performed this healing process, his manner was calm, and this was reflected in his speech and his body.

After six months of developing a relationship and greater stability in his home and school life, James' speech and dialogue began to make huge strides. He frequently addressed me directly, and, although still using very short, command-like sentences, those around him commented on the variety of words he now used. During my sessions with James, I felt something of a paradox. He was a child who had isolated himself both physically and emotionally from the people around him, and yet he had become almost universally liked. In contradiction to his violent behaviour, people warmed to him and he tended to be discussed in favourable terms. As his language changed, a range of emotional experiences developed alongside. This enabled James to add to his existing history and influenced the way he understood himself and the world around him. As James transformed, so, too, did his father, who expanded his own understanding of the dichotomy of the previous good–bad split with which he had viewed his children. This was revealed throughout the regular review sessions we were able to have. As James demonstrated new behaviours, his father was able to view him in a new light. Suddenly, expectations, which appeared to be fixed and rigid, had become more flexible. This threw open possibilities for many aspects of his father's life to change and, in particular, the way he related to James. He began to question this relationship much more, and this led to him becoming much more physically affectionate towards James. As his expectations changed, he saw James in a new light.

In class, James was encouraged to share and play with his peers, not simply alongside them. When visiting his class about a year into our time working together, I watched as another child was sharing out a plate of biscuits I believe they had all made together earlier in the day. Each child, including James, had already taken one when, unseen by the boy carrying the plate, one biscuit fell to the floor. I watched, half expecting James to quickly eat the biscuit, or hide it for later. Instead, he tapped the boy on the shoulder and placed it back on the plate. Compared to when I had first met James, this felt like significant progress.

It would be easy to identify James as a child caught within very primitive stages of infant development. It would be difficult, and similarly unproductive, to try to discover how much of his language and cognitive difficulties are attributable to his autism and how much may have been the result of some emotional and physical deprivation during his early years. James was simply James. This is whom I had to work with. Within a psychoanalytic framework, James could be identified akin to a preverbal infant caught within the early stages of viewing the world through polarized perspectives. Klein (1988) identified clear terms for this good–bad split in her "paranoid–schizoid position", prior to a realization through experience of the spectrum of responses in between. In this theoretical model, the primary care-giver is caught by the projections of the developing infant, and, for James, this was strongly paralleled in the experiences of his father.

Fundamentally, however, the only way for James to change his behaviour in relationships was through experiencing one. His view of the world had been essentially tarnished by the early negativity he had experienced. His way of relating to people was one of fear and scepticism, and yet, at the same time, he seemed to exude a warmth, perhaps indicative of a need for some support and affection. When James' father was able to provide this, it seemed to meet a need in both of them. Through forming an experience of a new relationship in the therapy room, it presented an opportunity for disclosure of very specific emotional experiences within a new context.

Ultimately, I felt my role with James was often just letting him know whom I was, another person relating to him. By identifying myself as another existing being (a different person but in his image), able to relate to him, James' self-awareness and self-perception were able to grow. Existentially viewed, his self-awareness did not simply arrive overnight, and this process should not be perceived as something absent in a young child and then suddenly acquired. James, perhaps, had had his trust in his main nurturing and care-giving adults taken from him, first by his mother's struggle with alcohol, and second, by being taken from her care. It was no surprise, then, that his fear predominated, causing even greater withdrawal from social and emotional relatedness. In my work with James, I was able to create shared experiences and, hence, opportunities for specific personal disclosures, such as how I felt with him at certain times, or how I experienced our relationship alongside specific actions he took. In bandaging the imaginary wounds I had sustained in our sessions together, I was able to demonstrate not only the experience of my own pain, but also encourage a reflective awareness that he was, in fact, able to inflict such an experience. This, in turn, became increasingly emotive for James. Through these disclosures, I hoped to humanize myself in our relationship and begin to alter the specula image he saw of himself in the mirror. Only by a growth of his awareness of relatedness and being-with-others could James begin to identify an authentic sense of himself.

CHAPTER EIGHT

Existential phenomenology

Jacob

Jacob was a child I saw for eighteen months, who was six years old when we began our work together. He was referred to me as a child in "need" of psychotherapy by his social worker. Throughout much of his life, he had been an unfortunate witness to the violent and often drunken abuse his father directed towards his mother. His only respite from this volatile environment appeared to be when his father went "missing" for several days, even weeks, at a time. Just prior to him being referred to me, however, his father had been arrested and charged with assault after his mother had gained the confidence to involve the police, and a social worker had quickly been appointed.

I always looked forward to my sessions with Jacob. Although often sombre and, indeed, rarely laughing or smiling, he carried with him an air of maturity and sophistication which belied his age and circumstances. He was six years old, but conversed with me in a very adult way, and I often reflected to colleagues in supervision that if he were twenty or thirty years older, he could almost be a friend. During the beginning of our work together, Jacob chose to play little, instead preferring to sit and chat about the events of his week and what he had done, generally in a quite factual manner. He would tell me what he ate, what lessons he enjoyed at school, and so on, rarely mentioning his family relationships or his emotional response to recent events, even when prompted to do so.

The focus of discussion during our eighteenth session together was around whether or not I had any children of my own, or whether I lived with any children at home. I had initially tried to explore his enquiries in an overly theoretical way, asking what it might be like if there indeed were other children at my home, and reminding him that he did already know I saw other children for psychotherapy. Later, I considered how this seemed to be the first time he had directly asked "me" a question, and the first time I felt challenged with him. Thus far, Jacob had somehow managed our sessions, in a sense. He chose to keep himself and me safe. Through directly acknowledging my outside life and humanity, it felt as if something new in the dialogue had been created. I experienced Jacob as beginning to see an element of humanity that was different to the previously professional and courteous relationship. The choice of engaging in a new way carried with it a risk, and I understood Jacob's questions as explorative, testing out, within our dialogue, how committed I was to engaging and not letting him down in a way that perhaps others historically had.

The following session, Jacob arrived in a playful mood, and, although I chose to reflect with him upon some of the questioning of the previous week, he decided not to develop it further. Instead, we worked on drawing a face and painting a mask. During the painting, Jacob enjoyed mixing the colours and squirting the paint. He drew the face carefully and took his time in selecting colours for the mask. While he painted, we talked, and he told me about his family: his sister, whom he found boring, and his baby brother, who slept in his mother's bed, ". . . well you know where babies sleep . . .", and of his step-brother, who lived abroad. He also spoke about his father, who lived down a motorway with flashing lights, a thousand miles away, which makes you fall asleep. Jacob left the session smiling, and asked to lock the door to the therapy room himself.

Towards the end of our work, I remember both of us reflecting on the time we spent together, and the way our perceptions of each other had changed and evolved. I have a strong memory of Jacob telling me that to begin with he thought I would judge him, perhaps telling him off if he made mistakes, but had later realized that we were able to play and talk together without the need for "right" or "wrong" answers.

Over the year and a half I spent working with him, many themes emerged; his reserved, often quiet appearance, his outward emotional control, which had clearly developed over time, and a desire to control the depth of relationships, perhaps having become quite self-sufficient to maintain his own safety. The most powerful disclosures I was offered from Jacob were, however, around my own feelings and responses when I sat with him. How did he make me feel? What did this reveal about our relationship and my understanding of his world-view? I include myself in the relationships I have with my clients, and this is key to an understanding that is revealed through our dialogue. The wisdom that can be present in the play of both therapist and client is for me intensely conspicuous when working with children.

In this brief example, it is possible to see the importance and value of my being in "relation to" Jacob: his recognition of me as another person in the room with him, and not simply a professional without family or context, seemed to mark a significant shift in our relationship. It appeared to me that Jacob had become an important emotional carer in the family home, not only for himself, but also, as he later revealed, for his mother. The idea of being able to play with an adult was a very new concept for him, and somehow an important experience for me, too. It highlighted the challenge of engaging with each child in a way that does not involve bracketing my knowledge of their context or history, but acknowledging how it informs our unique dialogue created in each session.

Heidegger and phenomenology

Phenomenology is discourse, and, as I now attempt the difficult task of describing and explaining my understanding of Heideggerian phenomenology as a psychotherapeutic method, I should be aware of the contradiction that lies in that very statement. First, Heidegger did not intend his explanation of phenomenology to be used as a psychotherapeutic method. Second, he did not intend it to be a doctrine. It was merely his means of investigation.

> Phenomenology neither designates the object of its researches, nor characterizes the subject-matter thus comprised. The word merely informs us of the "how" with which what is to be treated in this science gets exhibited and handled. [Heidegger, 2000, p. 59]

He tells us here that, unlike other, more scientific methods of analysis, phenomenology does not tell us in what way or where to direct our research, but that it will modestly inform us of the "how", the very means by which what we look at comes to light. What is revealed is how we are unable to escape the preconceptions our world brings with it.

In his explanation, Heidegger chose to trace the concept of phenomenology back to its original Greek etymology, which I shall discuss below. He also acknowledged the work of both Immanuel Kant and Edmund Husserl, the latter to whom he dedicated his book, *Being and Time.*

Kant described a distinction between "noumena" and "phonoumena" through his example of a horse. He suggested that when we think of a horse, the image we imagine is that of a thoroughbred race horse—a shiny coat, a plaited mane, in short, the quintessential image of a horse. This is often a very different appearance to the actual experience of coming face to face with a real horse. For Kant, the true essence, or noumena, of an object was unobtainable, something to be strived for and, essentially not apparent in our real life. The real life experience of a horse may have a bad odour, a patchy coat, and tangled mane. The distinction that he made is between an essential quality of "things" and the actuality of experience. This logical notion informs us of a "true" reality of different objects in life which we encounter in their imperfect state.

Heidegger also passes comment on the reality of experience, but not with the same objective distinction. For Heidegger, there is always a context; we are always in the world and "the world" is always constitutive of our very being. As *Dasein*, an "intentionality" is essential to our existence. In other words, we are always directed towards the world and to possibility. It is not possible for us to choose to see the world, or objects in it, in an isolated and objective way, perhaps moving to and fro, assessing a notion of "world" from both inside and out.

When Heidegger wrote about the things he described as "ready-to-hand", he expressed how the essential qualities of a hammer cannot be grasped by merely knowing that it works in conjunction with nails and hits other objects. The true nature and characteristics of the hammer are learnt from actually using it, hitting something and feeling the vibrations. Our actual knowledge of the object comes from experience and interacting with it. The hammer is equipment for us because it is understood as a hammer. This means we have a twofold relation to the hammer: the tangible process of experience and understanding which comes from its use, and also the prereflective understanding we have that it is, indeed, a hammer. We do not see it as an ambiguous object, and whether it is used to hit a nail, a nut, or a thumb, we need not deliberate over its use. Because of our personal and cultural history, the hammer is a tool used to strike things with. The knowledge and understanding we have of objects and tools, in the world, allows us to cope with everyday life. We need not interpret every aspect of our waking life that we encounter, and its use: when driving my car, I do not have to go through an identification process of recognizing the key as a key, or the lock as a lock, in order to open the door. Instead, I am simply able to open the door, probably with my thoughts already projected forwards towards my destination or the time I have to reach it. In *Being and Time*, Heidegger explains how we only become aware of many of these objects as "what they are" through encounters of difficulty: in other words, when the object breaks. If the key breaks in the lock, if I take the wrong key, if the lock is frozen in the cold morning frost, then in my awareness it becomes a lock. This dialogue of coping and awareness in our everyday lives is an important one for understanding how it is that we relate to the world around us. Indeed, an understanding of being with others in the world is similarly related to language and how our understanding leads to knowledge. The therapeutic importance of language and understanding when working with children is discussed further in Chapter Ten.

Husserl's phenomenology

Like Heidegger, Edmund Husserl before him also disagreed with dualistic traditions of a subject–object world in which both man and the world around him could be encountered and understood as separate entities. Husserl believed the only knowledge we as humans could have any certainty over was that which we accomplished through our own conscious experience. Consequently, he did not address the existence of an *a priori* essence of each object we encounter. This viewpoint really avoids the question of the existence of a reality of truths separate to us, but conveys to us that knowledge is, essentially, drawn from experience.

From this premise, the phenomenology of Husserl moves towards a methodology based around the notion of description. His phenomenology could perhaps be described as the qualities of what it is that is disclosed to us at any given moment, and, in some ways, negates the ambiguities inherent in understanding.

Husserl's phenomenological method was drawn from the conclusion that our experience of the world is singularly our own construct, "containing both directional (noematic) and referential (noetic) foci" (Spinelli, 1989, p. 16). In effect, he built up a system for the exploration of our knowledge of the things we experience. The outcome could, consequently, not be a "pure" essential understanding of whatever was in question, but could still be a rigorous investigation. For Husserl, then, the inconsistencies of our experiences could be illuminated and purified and understood intentionally, or as a reference point for experience. The method itself comprised three steps: the rule of *Epoche*, the rule of *Description*, and the rule of *Horizontalization* (see Spinelli, 1989).

Suppose that all speculation and presumptions that you made were always correct. You would maybe find yourself leading a life in which you would know the outcome of all decisions and dilemmas. This would invariably make you a hugely successful person. Now imagine a life in which you thought that every speculation or interpretation that you made was correct, but it was not. This would perhaps result in a complete polarity of the first scenario—a disastrous life, causing detriment to yourself and the people around you. The rule of *Epoche* encourages us to suspend judgements, and "bracket" our own personal assumptions. This is intended to open us up to possibility, from where we must then restrain the temptation to interpret our perceived experiences. This is achieved through the rule of *Description*. The third challenge Husserl sets us is in not establishing within our thoughts a hierarchy of presented experiences (*Horizontalization*). The temptation within most therapeutic work is to establish an immediate recognition of how important or salient a child's comments are to our own perception of the focus of their therapy. We may, for example, consider a bereaved child discussing the death of a relative as inherently more significant than an issue of feeling bullied or isolated at school. These assumptions, however, are our own. Husserl's phenomenology, therefore, aimed to bypass, as it were, the possibility of incorrect interpretation and presupposition. He concentrated purely on the descriptive process of life at a *pre-theoretical* stage, and his phenomenology can be looked upon as the detailed description of conscious experience, without making conscious reference to explanation and interpretation.

Understanding and interpretation

The idea of descriptive phenomenology is, as Heidegger tells us "tautological", as the qualities of what defines itself in our encounter with an object is the very dialogue that lies within the concept of phenomenology. The process of interpretation that Husserl tried so hard to negate was, for Heidegger, inherent in the paradigm of his phenomenology. The dialogue that exists in phenomenology involves our interpretation and understanding at its very core, and it is seemingly impossible to ignore our own interpretation of an object or an event. It is not something that we voluntarily choose; it is impossible for me to look at a chair and not know, or at least be aware of, some of the qualities that it has. In the same way, when I am with a child, it is impossible not to feel sorrow if I am genuinely moved by the presentation of their distress or circumstances. It may not always be appropriate to react with a display of sadness to the child in a psychotherapeutic session, but it should not be suppressed or ignored. If we aim to conduct any way of being with a child that is going to make an acknowledgement of Heideggerian phenomenology, it must take note of precisely the emotions, interpretations, and reactions that are brought to light.

On examining the etymology of the word "phenomenology", we find it can be broken down into two concepts from the original Greek meaning: "phos" and "logos". Phos is light, in this sense, the "bringing to light" of things. Logos has many interpretations, including telling a tale, exhibiting, making a statement, laying out, and, most commonly for Heidegger, "discourse". The "bringing to light" could be described as the manner by which things come to light and show themselves, such as a chair, which may be in front of us, shows itself as a chair: as discussed previously, this is not something that we have any control over, it is not something that carries with it meaning. What is important is the "chairness" of the chair, and, most decisively, how we become aware of that. The exhibiting of something, such as the chair, is exhibited in "relatedness", or the discourse or manner with which we address ourselves to the chair.

It is important to note that the discourse that I am describing is not verbal. It is a relationship. It is a "relationship to", an interrelation between us and the world around us. Phenomenology discloses, and uncovers. It "does violence" to the everyday assumptions that we have: it deconstructs history. Heidegger describes it as the process "to let that which shows itself be seen from itself in the very way in which it shows itself from itself" (2000, p. 58).

But this brief summation, although something of a tongue-twister, is an inappropriate maxim on its own. To be told that something will show itself from itself is not the experience, and certainly not a dialogue. If I am going to try to describe any type of phenomenological account, it must involve the reader. It must be a personalized account of *my* understanding of the process and something that as a reader you should address and interpret. In the same way, it is the integral nature of the *relationship* which is at the heart of what existential phenomenology attempts to do, which is,

> to characterize the nature of a person's experience of his world and himself. It is not so much an attempt to describe particular objects of his existence as to set all particular experiences within the context of his whole being-in-the-world. [Laing, 1990, p. 17]

Patrick

Patrick was eight years old when he began to see me for psychotherapeutic work together. The sessions took place once a week in a therapy room at his school. His mother had explained how she suffered with depression off and on for many years following the sudden death of her father at a young age. She previously had a difficult relationship with him, which she never seemed able to recover from. Her depression had affected Patrick from a young age, and, although they bonded well, she relied on him heavily and rarely left the family home. He was also absent from school on a regular basis, and this was a cause for concern. His mother had recently decided that the best way for them to find a solution to her unrest was to move back to her home town in the north of England. Meanwhile, Patrick's mother was very open and keen for him to come and see me before this occurred.

Patrick was always pleasant and polite but, when attending our sessions, I often found him displaying a noticeably heavy and serious expression on his face, almost dejected. He was receptive to attending and entering into a new relationship with me, always responding to my interventions, but normally in a very literal manner. In short, Patrick seemed unused to playing, almost anxious in an environment in which he could express his emotional experiences of the world, and be listened to.

In the fifth session, Patrick decided that he would like to draw. He took a cardboard box down from the shelf and a large tub of felt-tip pens and he began to sketch. As he drew, he explained the scene to me with very little intervention or prompting from myself. He drew a small tree stump in the middle of the box, which he described as a "dark magic tree" with spikes, and he sketched a sad mouth with large fangs protruding from it. The tree looked very sinister to me, and I commented on this to Patrick. Around the tree he drew lots of clouds and lines that he described as wind. These completely encircled the small tree. Then the clouds started to rain, and Patrick had said that there was a strong danger of the tree being blown over. I had suggested that there were no gaps in the clouds at all and that there didn't appear to be any sun. Patrick replied that there was one small place near the tree, and he drew a small circular squiggle, that was a "magical spot" and that this could possibly save the tree. This appeared to be just a small glimmer of hope for the tree, despite the strong winds and its complete encirclement. Patrick also talked about how everything in his life was going to be wonderful when he moved to the north of England, and at the same time he expressed real and earnest concern, as he hoped he would still come to the therapy room and be able to see me. Patrick's story then ended abruptly and he said that he wanted to play with something else. When I asked him about the conclusion of the story, he told me that he didn't know yet, and we decided that maybe we would return to the tree at a later date.

Patrick's narrative and images provoked me. His unhappy, despondent presentation evoked in me feelings of protection and a desire to want to rescue him. Perhaps in some prereflective manner, this is the world-view of himself that Patrick projected out towards adults in his company: "rescue me". At the same time, throughout the session described, it is possible to see how Patrick expressed, through creative means for the very first time how he, like his mother looked for outside solutions to his own downheartedness. For his mother, salvation lay in a geographical move, while for Patrick's tormented tree, hope was at that point in a small, almost overlooked magic spot. I was encouraged, however, by his continued desire to attend our sessions, even though it was clearly a very new and sometimes challenging place for him to be. I felt it was important for me to be aware of my urge to want to rescue him, but, at the same time, not act on this and take away his responsibility. If he were to rely on me for his rescue or escape, he would be denied the opportunity of further understanding the threat of the clouds around him and remain encircled by them for much longer. Without understanding the threats he perceived and always relying on my knowledge to address them, Patrick would inevitably remain vulnerable and in need of rescue by someone else.

Often, in life, it seems preferable to look for external blame for our own emotions, and, similarly, easier to look externally for a solution. The expectation of a "cure" or "answer" to a child's presentation is a common reason for them to be referred to me for therapy. The reality, however, is something much more challenging, and, in being able to grasp their own individual role in how they experience the world, children, and adults around them, they are already making a huge leap forward in recognizing the potential for change.

Interpretations we make, whether they are verbalized or not, give rise to possibility. In suggesting, or even defining, an emotional response that a child may experience, it is possible for them to then further their own understanding and possibilities by considering it and agreeing or disagreeing. Whether the interpretation is correct or not becomes almost, although not completely, immaterial. A child in a session, during a moment of pathos, may, for example, be told that he appears saddened by what has been said. This provides the child with the opportunity to consider the process he or she has just experienced: was it sadness, or something else? This, in turn, provides an opportunity for the possibility of new, genuine, and truthful understanding for the child. In this circumstance, interpreting and defining can be liberating, and both act as deliverers of possibilities, not limiting elements in a psychotherapeutic relationship.

Traditionally, defining experiences could be seen as a process limiting possibilities, but, as I have now tried to explain, this is not necessarily the case. The openness to possibility lies in the manner in which interpretations are made, and the sincere and open-minded intent in their delivery. If, for example, we say that the emotional expression of a child *is* something, then we are limiting what it could be only to the range of things that could be understood by the particular words that we select. We are, by proxy, suggesting not only that it is something, but that it is also not something else. In therapy, this helps us to place the focus back on to the individual to encourage the child to question ways in which they may choose to define or understand themselves (e.g., vulnerable and the victim of bullying, or confident and well liked by all their peers). It could be possible to say that when we define ourselves or our beliefs, if the two are different, then we are limiting ourselves to possibilities beyond the boundaries of these created objective truths.

An evaluation of the definitions, subsequent to experiences that we all take for granted, could ideally lead to a process that could bring about greater possibility through awareness. If we question what we have taken for granted in our lives up to a given point, then such questions paradoxically become answers. As answers and truths, which have limits and edges, they act as regressing our awareness next to questions. As a therapist, this type of investigation and reflection I hope can at least start to bring about relevant questions.

One of the most important factors within these ideas of phenomenological practice is the awareness the therapist has of their own experience with a child. The shared undertaking that occurs is represented through how their experience is shared with the child, and the communication that exists between them in the intention that they have towards that specific child at that time. How the therapist may feel when sitting with a particular child is perhaps the most honest and reliable interpretation they are able to make. Some children may be exciting to be with, and these may be sessions the therapist looks forward to with great anticipation. Others may demand more of the therapist and the time may pass very slowly. What qualities make some children exceptionally vulnerable and provoke feelings of needing to be rescued? How the therapist feels with each child reveals some aspects of their experiences and ultimately their world. If I, as the therapist, feel I want to rescue them and take them away to a "better" life, what might this be disclosing about their experiences at home or school, and their history, which has brought them to this manner of being?

CHAPTER NINE

Knowing and not knowing: existential perspectives on truth

The archaeological paradigm within psychoanalysis, in which the therapist adopts a role of explorer, seeking for the "hidden" latent truth in a child's presenting pathology or narrative, does not hold true for existential practice. When presented with the playful and creative narrative of a child, a traditional psychoanalytic model of practice may encourage the therapist to distinguish between the surface presentation and a deeper underlying truth. It becomes a necessary part of the therapeutic process to endeavour to uncover the true meaning of what is actually being revealed by the child. The objects presented lose their surface meaning, turning into symbols of deeper representation.

At a very simplistic level, a toy animal figure stuck in the sand, for example, could be interpreted as representing the troubled mother paralysed by her own anxiety and fear. The figure is not just a figure, but becomes imbued with additional meaning and symbolism beyond what it actually is. When working through an existential–phenomenological framework, this distinction is unnecessary and unhelpful. Instead, the presentation of the child and their story can simply be understood as a truthful representation in itself. Any greater understanding, which the therapist may strive for, arrives subsequently, not through the interpretation of a theoretical framework or scientific knowledge, but from an establishment of ever-widening contexts. In the case of the toy figure in the child's narrative, this may be a matter of considering what type of toy this is. Perhaps it is a wild or domesticated one. Perhaps the child has chosen a different figure to last time. This, in turn, raises questions about how the child may view and perceive this animal, and the sensation of it being stuck. A mutual understanding is developed through the phenomenological disclosure of the choice of animal, its context, and so forth. As the context and understanding expand, so, in some ways, do the choices and possibilities. This process of existential practice does not establish a system for interpretation, but a context for understanding, which includes the world as a whole. The meanings of each toy chosen to construct the child's narrative already arrive in the play with values that may or may not be explicitly acknowledged, but are, none the less, present. The child may use a toy lion as a mother, but it is still initially a lion, unless we are told otherwise.

Knowing the world

Upon reading Heidegger's primary text, *Being and Time*, it becomes clear that he did not intend us to adopt his understanding of the world as a doctrine for life, or even to adopt his exploration of ontology as a methodology for psychotherapy. Within the text lies a discourse, a stubborn obstinacy, if you will, that encourages us, as readers, to think for ourselves. Within the text there is always the material, what is said, and, at the same time, there is the process, the reflective and unreflective dialogue. He states that discourse is a function of our very "Being": "Knowing the world . . .—or rather addressing oneself to the 'world' and discussing it (logos)—thus functions as the primary mode of Being-in-the-world, even though Being-in-the-world does not as such get conceived" (Heidegger, 2000, p. 85).

When Heidegger talks here of "knowing" the world, he is introducing a relationship, not suggesting that the world is something that we are able to grasp a knowledge of by fitting it into some kind of classification. His idea of addressing oneself to the world is through "concern". He is suggesting here that we do not think of ourselves philosophically, in a primordial sense in relation to "Being-in-the-world", and, indeed, he goes on to state that this structure as a whole remains ontologically inaccessible to us. Instead, we relate to our "Being" as a whole through our relationships to other people and objects, of which the world is constituted, and discussing them. The "Being" of entities can, as Heidegger claims (*ibid.*, p. 59), be covered up, although this Being belongs somehow to the entity that shows itself, and does so in such an integral way that it constitutes its meaning. Thus, what shows itself is the Being of the entity, even when it is "covered up so extensively that it becomes forgotten". Subsequently, things may demand to be seen and show themselves in a distinctive sense, revealing the characteristics that make them what they are.

As has already been established, we cannot understand ourselves in isolation. An understanding of Being can only be sought through relatedness, and one such example is the therapeutic relationship. Similarly, in "knowing" the world or "understanding" a child's circumstances, the therapist is not the expert. Nor should he or she try to adopt this role. The "knowledge" given in understanding is not a form of absolute, objectified truth. The therapist is not a teacher. They simply have the task of laying the foundations and establishing the context in which a troubled child may become more aware of their possibilities.

Existential psychotherapy probably does not involve a discussion of complex philosophy with a client of any age. An explicit exploration of their understanding of the meaning of Being would clearly be extremely unproductive with a young child. Instead, an ontological understanding of our existence is revealed through our relationships. It is through the opening up of a child's existing relationships that potential is created for understanding. If a "cause" or reason is sought by the therapist for a child's behaviour, the effect is narrowing, not opening up, and the possibility of broadening understanding may be lost.

Elizabeth

Her reception class teacher referred Elizabeth at just five years old. She attended a mainstream state primary school, but her behaviour had been deemed so bad that several parents had petitioned the headteacher to have her excluded and threatened to withdraw their own children from school.

At the point of referral, Elizabeth was living with her grandparents, as her mother, who had left Britain to elope with her partner, had abandoned her eighteen months before. Elizabeth's dad lived nearby, and had regular contact with her at weekends. When leaving for another country, her mother had simply written a note and left one night. After several meetings with Elizabeth's grandparents and her class teacher, I began to have one-to-one sessions with Elizabeth in a room in school designated for counselling or therapy. She was always exceptionally keen to attend her weekly sessions, and would frequently run out of class to see me before it was time for our session.

Her behaviour was initially very controlling towards me, and, as she explored the room and the art materials that I had brought, she directed almost all of my involvement in our dialogue. "I'm going to draw my family and you're going to draw me . . . and then I'll be the teacher and you can be in the class." She regularly chose to adopt the role of other adults in her life, particularly her teacher, and this provided an opportunity for us to explore her relationships and perceptions. During one session, Elizabeth had discussed how she liked to sleep in her grandmother's bed and in the morning she would have to see her grandmother immediately, for reassurance. If her grandmother was in the shower when Elizabeth awoke, she said she would just shout for her and keep shouting until she arrived. We explored the reasons why she wished to be so close to her grandmother, particularly when going to sleep, and Elizabeth vividly described her experience of believing unknown "scary" figures may be lurking in dark. Having explained the fears and anxiety she had experienced through this dark, shadowy, ethereal character, I asked if she could draw him. Elizabeth told me that she didn't know what he looked like, and, in her own language, that she felt unable to make bedtime feel safer. As we spoke, she appeared to feel more anxious in the room during our session. At this point, I reminded her of the control she was normally able to exercise, both in the room, through a freedom of expression, and also in our relationship, by dictating so much of our play.

Elizabeth took a piece of paper and began, in her own way, to write what she described as a letter. Although she asked me to help her spell and sound out words, the composition was entirely her own and read as follows: "To Scary Man Ian, go away and never come back From Elizabeth and Chris." Underneath these words she drew a long thin rectangle, later naming this as a gun, held by a tall stick figure with long hair. Elizabeth described the figure as her mother, who was holding the gun. Upon the gun she drew "pictures of babies", which made the gun "stronger" and more powerful. This gun, she added, would be able to kill the scary man and keep her safe. She drew and decorated the letter very carefully and appeared to be extremely proud of it at the end of her session. She then asked if I could take the picture and show it to her class teacher.

Elizabeth continued to attend sessions with me for a further year. As the sessions continued, many of her fears and anxieties slowly ebbed away. Over time, more and more she chose to discuss issues relating to her peer group in class, arguments they had together, and games from which she felt excluded. Although Elizabeth grew in confidence during our sessions, later allowing me greater opportunity to challenge her control of our dialogue, her behaviour in class continued to be disruptive. Importantly, however, she stayed in school, and was not excluded, as had been requested by the parents of several other children in her class. Our sessions, however, came to an unplanned and unsatisfactory end when her mother returned from abroad, pregnant with her second child, and it was not long before Elizabeth went to live with her.

Elizabeth was a young girl who had undoubtedly been greatly affected by the loss of a close relationship with her mother at a crucial point in her development. The impact of this loss was clear to see in the anxiety she experienced each night at bedtime, and then again in her search for the reassuring presence of her grandmother each morning. From an existential perspective, many of Elizabeth's fears came from being alone. Even when she was with her grandmother, the potential to be abandoned again was always present. It came as no surprise to me that she was consequently so keen to attend our sessions each week, in which we were able to establish a consistent and regular pattern of expectation. From this, she was able to explore her own understanding of her relationship with me and also of those other people who were significant in her life. Her very ontological existence was shaped and defined by the relationships she experienced on a day-to-day basis. It was these relationships that shaped her Being, and the manner through which she experienced the world—in essence, her world-view.

It would have been unproductive to linger on the causes of Elizabeth's distress, or to uncover subsequent pathologies. Instead, we focused on her experience of her own anxieties and, equally, her experience of our relationship. Despite her circumstances, this revealed the opportunity for new possibilities and Elizabeth was able to regain some control of her fears. To pathologize Elizabeth's presenting behaviour or history would, in fact, have had the opposite effect of creating an illness or set of symptoms that would have made her feel even more helpless. However tragic life events may be, they are always accompanied by choices: these choices may be somewhat limited, but it is their very existence which allows a child in therapy to see the possibilities of how they can be.

Truth and truthfulness

Scientific knowledge has overtaken the traditional pursuit for what Heidegger (1987, p. 26) refers to as a "theory of knowledge". He claims that western metaphysics has pursued the quest for a "theory of knowledge" from as far back as Aristotle, Plato, and Parmenides. This motivation for the seeking out of knowledge is typified by Kant's famous definition of reason,

> In accordance with reason's legislative prescriptions, our diverse modes of knowledge must not be permitted to be a mere rhapsody, but must form a system. Only so can they further the essential ends of reason. By a system I understand the unity of the manifold modes of knowledge under one idea. This idea is the concept provided by reason—of the form of the whole—in so far as the concept determines a priori not only the scope of its manifold content, but also the positions which the parts occupy relatively to one another. [Kant, 1964, pp. 653ff]

Here, according to Kant, reason is so objectified that it effects its own "legislative" power over knowledge in its formation of a system. For him, knowledge must be unified under a system in order to be understood and utilized. For Heidegger, this, I imagine, would be typical of a western tradition that takes knowledge to be the behaviour and attitude of representation by which what is true is to be grasped and maintained as something that can be possessed. In Heidegger's discussion of the work of Nietzsche, *The Will to Power as Knowledge and as Metaphysics* he goes on to suggest that "What is true and its possession—or, more succinctly, truth in the sense of thing's being recognized as true—constitute the essence of knowledge" (1987, p. 24).

Knowledge, he continues, is fundamentally enquiring about truth and its essence. What is held up and taken to be true, then, essentially, is. It is necessary here to make an important split between truth and truthfulness. Truth, as it has been used here, is generally used to describe an objective world. Emotions are, for example, lent more easily to an assessment of truthfulness, as opposed to being true or false, and the experiences of emotions are certainly not things that can be objectively quantified and defined. If I experienced a feeling of anger that I then reflected upon, I would not be able to say the experience was truly anger, in a definitive sense, which would apply to all subsequent experiences of anger. Conversely, it would be wrong to suggest the experience was, therefore, false, and not a true understanding of anger, as it certainly exhibited strong parallels with the experiences of anger I had previously been aware of. A more accurate way of assessing this emotion would be to consider whether it could be judged to be genuine and honest or, indeed, truthful. The expression of the emotion could, thus, be identified through the examination of truthfulness and could be said to have intended to be sincere or deceptive.

Heidegger draws upon the remark made by Nietzsche "that honouring truth is already the consequence of an illusion" (cited in Heidegger, 1987, p. 24). Truth, although demanded and honoured by man, is, he suggests, essentially an illusion. The honouring of truth and an objectifiable quest for what is real are also present in the work of Plato. In the *Symposium*, he describes how Socrates engages in dialogue about the true nature of love, and how within truth exists the judgement of what is good.

> "The only subject of men's love is what is good. Don't you agree?" "Certainly I do." "May we then say without qualification that men

> are in love with what is good?" "Yes." "But we must add, mustn't we, that the aim of their love is the possession of the good for themselves?" "Yes." "And not only its possession but its perpetual possession?" "Certainly." "To sum up, then, love is desire for the perpetual possession of the good." "Very true.' [Plato, 1957, p. 86]

Love, here, is seen as something that can be strived for, and that man has an inherent drive for the possession of what is "good". Love, conversely, can be considered as something poetic and artful. From both Plato and Heidegger, it is possible to become aware of a tendency to rely on existing definitions and truths. An honouring of truth, it seems, can lead us towards something that is verifiable and can be judged as good or bad. Love, however, as a poetic word, becomes art, as it is a word that creates—it forces us to consider circumstances, and does not, for me, contain any form of right or wrong. Love, like the disturbance of experience, brings to light something novel and, like art, it stands in opposition to truth and its illusory qualities. Art cannot be classified, and, as Nietzsche claims, "we have art in order not to perish from the truth" (cited in Heidegger, 1987, p. 822). Art, like experience then, can claim to bring about awareness from the newness of dialogue, but it is not true to say that truth, or certainly the pursuit for the possession of it, has no relevance for psychotherapy.

I would even go as far as to suggest that, for many people today, the advancement of names for symptoms and their subsequent diagnosis represents the furtherance of medicine and science.

Contrary to science, however, historicity does not allow for the absolute "prescribed truths" of authorities. A philosophical, more pluralistic split can be made, however, between scientific truth and personal truth. On one side lies modern science, with its rigid adherence to natural laws that cannot be broken, and on the other side lies postmodern thought, claiming that there is no such thing as absolute truth. Truth, for the latter, is always plural, and not what we may take to be generally accepted truth from an authority, which is socially constructed. As Derrida wrote, "There is no such thing as a truth in itself, but only a surfeit of it" (1979, p. 103).

However, as an existential psychotherapist, I think maybe the relevance of truth to knowledge lies somewhere between these two extremes. Within therapy, there should be no will-to-power that is present in so much scientific thought, since this is simply a focusing of knowledge of the object. On the other hand, it would ultimately be nihilistic to follow the postmodern argument that Derrida advocates: if the world of truths were entirely personal and ephemeral, what role would there be for the therapeutic possibilities of intersubjectivity? With such a pluralistic view in mind, the involvement of another person and their opinions would lose its value and its ability to disrupt and disturb.

Maybe it is the very pursuit itself that is relevant for psychotherapy—a transcendental process of daring to be bold. This is a personal process for the child, their family, and one that somehow includes the therapist. The therapist John Heaton described an example of this personal process that can also include someone else in different circumstances, in reflecting on his experiences of Laing:

> The soul is great according the measure of this flame and of its sadness, the good is the good only in sadness. For the spirit divides. These thoughts of Heidegger's on spirit are intensely reminiscent of Augustine and Augustine reminds me of Laing. One of my last and vivid memories of him is soon after he had left his second wife and was in deep distress, Barbara and I asked him round to dinner. He came with a volume of Augustine and we spent from 10pm to 4am discussing Augustine's notion of evil. "Audacity—that is sin." This is the process of coming into being, the first differentiation, the will of the soul to belong to itself rather than God. The relation of this notion of evil to the dialectics of the self was one of Laing's favourite themes. [Heaton, 1995, pp. 80–81]

The poetic and moving nature of this brief passage, and, indeed, the entire article, evoke an awareness of what is revealed not only about Heidegger, Augustine, and Laing, but also most saliently about John Heaton. The importance of knowledge for existential psychotherapy is not related to method or systems, but to wisdom that allows us to see the whole of an encounter and not simply its constituent parts. With this wisdom, the therapist is able to include themselves in the relationships they have with the children they work with and, one hopes, allow *play* to steal a more central role than theory. The wisdom that can be present in the play of both therapist and child is, for me, intensely conspicuous when working with children.

Being is revealing

When something is revealed, or brought to light therapeutically, it is not, I believe, information or diagnosis provided by one person for another, but "inspiration", newness that is found in dialogue. As Heaton wrote,

> A hiddenness must be maintained in order that there be disclosure, a forgetfulness in order that there be memory. Only thus can the authentic word come—inspiration—rather than words being manipulated by the subject to produce what he already knows. [2001, p. 103]

The newness, or inspiration, is not a product of only talking, although it may be; it is not a product of silence, although it may be; it is not a product of simple understanding, although it may be, but it must be an individual process, even when we are in the company of others, and it must be a prereflective process.

Bearing this in mind, one may ask why existential phenomenology, or, indeed, why psychotherapy? If inspiration is a prereflective process, that is to say, it is created without meditative or contemplative recognition, why should I, as a psychotherapist, *try* to engage with the children I meet with professionally?

Within psychotherapeutic engagement lies discourse. And this discourse is the therapeutic nature of any psychotherapeutic encounter. If I hope, as a therapist, to encourage the children I work with to develop a greater understanding or awareness of themselves from the genesis of new knowledge, this will arise out of discourse and being in "relation to". Wolf similarly addressed the therapeutic nature of entering into a relationship when he wrote in the *Journal of the Society of Existential Analysis*, in response to a question he posed himself about why we would ask our therapist about Heidegger, which I believe included his asking how we question when we relate to ourselves and to others, and the therapeutic nature of "finding out about a relationship",

> Philosophy is a discourse, conversation, discussion, interaction, and is not about defining ideas and concepts. Philosophy is fundamentally a relationship, and a relationship which changes human life. I think that from here we can say that as a relationship which

> changes human life philosophy is therapeutic. Our relationship to Heidegger, our doing philosophy alongside Heidegger's text is fundamentally a therapeutic relationship which changes us, which brings us to see the world in a new way for the first time. [Wolf, 2000, p. 61]

"To see the world in a new way", could be stated as a fundamental of my existential–phenomenological psychotherapy, and I believe the "new" arises out of relationship, whether it is to a book (like Heidegger's text) or to a psychotherapist. It is important for me as a practitioner favouring a phenomenological emphasis, and as one working with children, to communicate directly with the individual and be aware of their potential within a therapeutic relationship. What I am considering here is not the same as an evangelical style, humanistic faith in the inherent healing ability of all human beings, but recognition of their possibilities. The relationship between client and therapist expressed through narrative is articulated by Minton: "it is the basis for the attempt to utilise our subjective experience of our worlds, and each other as part of those worlds, in order to facilitate an actualisation of the potential for growth and movement" (2000, p. 83).

As therapists, however, when we are in relationship with a child, is it possible to facilitate the child to become more aware of his or her self? I wonder, also, what the therapeutic significance of such self-knowledge may be, for it could well be a tricky line along which I tread, furthering their knowledge of themselves and their choices, but ensuring that they remain a part of society. At the end of each session with me, a child must, of course, return to their everyday life: in school; with their family; back to their carers; and so on. It is particularly true, when working with a child of any age, that the therapist must take some responsibility for their emotional state at the conclusion of the session. It would obviously be unsuitable to encourage a highly distressed child to just wander back into a crowded waiting area or a school playground, without providing an opportunity for them to prepare for life beyond the confines and therapeutic boundaries of the session. As well as the practical responsibilities that arrive with any process that may facilitate "self" knowledge or awareness, there is the ethical and philosophical dimension. It is simply insufficient to assume that a greater awareness of a child's situation and struggles in life is inherently therapeutic. Similarly, an ethically practising existential psychotherapist would not try to promote a process in which a child was re-experiencing difficult or abusive aspects of their history (in other words, simply retraumatizing them) with the hope that this may somehow prove cathartic. If such emotive content in a therapeutic session is to have value for a child, the awareness and progress will grow out of the reflective process, in dialogue.

One response to such dilemmas is to remember that as individuals, however inward or individualized, we must always think of ourselves as being in "relation to". This does not, however, shine light upon whether it is possible to raise this awareness in a conscious way with a child, or whether, indeed, it is necessary to go to therapy in order to enter into relational encounters.

Inward knowledge

Through his many publications, the nineteenth-century philosopher Søren Kierkegaard directly addressed notions of "inwardness", in many ways setting a template for the subsequent development of phenomenological psychology almost two hundred years later. His relation to modern phenomenology lies in a search for confirmation of meaning and sense in our own experience. Each experience, and the way we relate to it, unfolds from another experience.

Writing under the pseudonym Johannes Climacus, he suggested, in the book *Philosophical Fragments*, that awareness can be equated with Plato's doctrine of "recollection". As Plato suggests, learning could be described as a matter of the subject's becoming aware of what is present in his own mind. Kierkegaard (1992b) also indicated (in *Concluding Unscientific Postscript*) that it is the teacher's role to remind them of what they already possess. This could be true if the "truth" of knowledge lies not in information from without that can be grasped, but lies within. When an interpretation appears to fit comfortably, it is imperative that the ethical therapist asks himself or herself why.

In everyday life, it is easy to overlook where our sense of truth or knowledge may come from. When writing a letter, for example, I might find myself stuck in some way, searching for the word which best fits the sentiment I am trying to express. After further deliberation, I might believe that I have "found" the word which best fits. It seems in this situation that other similar words or phrases have been discarded, but it may also be apparent that no real search or thorough exploration has actually taken place. Yet, the word still "fits". Where does the sense of fitting actually come from? Clearly, there is no absolute thought here, no word that would be the absolutely perfect word to match that precise sentiment. What we have is an experience of first struggling, then appearing to find a word, and finally feeling contentment. In this particular, unique situation, the word simply felt like the correct one to express what I was tussling with. The experience and solution are directly related to the context, and the outcome could not have come solely from outside. Even if I had rifled through countless dictionaries to find a single word, the sense of how appropriate the words are can only come from the individual, in a given context. The "right" word sometimes seems strangely unobtainable, and yet simply the process of saying and describing the word I was trying to find enabled me to uncover a satisfactory answer. This raises questions as to whether it is the so-called "discovery" that is of importance, or some kind of investment in the process. This idea offers us interesting parallels to the psychotherapeutic process. Many children are thrown into a therapeutic relationship searching for a notion of truth. However, at some stage during our work together, the process of the search itself overtakes the significance of the answers, which may or may not be found.

Perhaps attending psychotherapy on a regular basis does not, in itself, inherently hold the key to a development of "newness" or a redeveloped personal awareness, but it could put a child in a position in which there lies a greater chance that something innovative may occur.

Personalized thought

So, how would it be possible to describe an accurate account of a personal discourse or dialogue with the world? How is it possible to direct a child to think for themselves, without irony? I am aware again that I am falling into my own trap, and the irony of encouraging individual, personalized process is self-contradictory. This is a lasting irony in much existential thought. While acknowledged by many philosophical thinkers, it is a notion conveniently overlooked by many existential psychotherapy practitioners who have tried, for example, to turn Heidegger's philosophy into a tool for therapeutic method. Kierkegaard, who, for many analytical thinkers, is not considered a true philosopher, spent much of his time addressing the task of encouraging independent and personalized thought (certainly for himself, if not always falling into the trap of ironically suggesting it for others). Throughout his writings, he fought against the abstracting of thought from existence. As I have already begun to address, the temptation to drift towards an objective understanding of children in a therapeutic relationship is a strong one. If both the process of understanding and the child whom we encounter in the therapy room are interpreted and experienced through a predetermined set of ideals or systems, then it may be impossible to remain truly open to the subsequent encounter and its context. Kierkegaard provides further clarification in his writing elsewhere: "When subjectivity, inwardness is the truth, the truth becomes objectively a paradox; and the fact that truth is objectively a paradox shows in its turn that subjectivity is the truth" (1992a, p. 223).

There exists, in his words here, a tension between a "subjectively" thoughtful individual person and their context and relation to the outside world. A subjective viewpoint draws its understanding of "truth" from a process of inwardness, and yet, from the outside, a personal "inward" process remains unquantifiable, indefinable, and, as Kierkegaard states, a paradox. It is necessary for us to engage and interpret our world in the context of already being in the world, and, hence, the tension of subjective truth and everyday living remains.

In this particular section of his work, Kierkegaard considers how truth may be found in subjectivity, and, as a therapist educated in the traditions of existential thought, for me it brings to light ideas surrounding the extent to which both psychotherapists and the children they work with are aware of their own subjective truths and, more importantly, their "striving" for these truths. (Here I am reminded of the idea of the religious preacher, Lessing, who described how if God were to hold truth in his right hand and the "life-long pursuit" of it in his left, he would have to choose the left.) It is, of course, not possible to follow an example of a "system", such as the subjective choice that Lessing provides for us in his sermon here, as the paradox of being told by someone else to find your own truth is almost as shocking as being able to see our own truth in front of us and simply grasp at it and obtain it.

Ideas of method and truth offer the refuge, or security, of knowledge. Whether it is in knowing or interpreting an alternate symbolic reality, or simply the reinforcement of a position of power, this is unhelpful and unnecessary. By the therapist adopting a position of expert, the child and their family may find themselves pushed into a role of unknowing victim. This positioning will inevitably reinforce the falsehood that change and choice relies on an outside force and not their own personal responsibility.

It is possible to be critical of anyone trying to turn Heidegger's concept of phenomenology into a method of psychotherapy, as it is not a transferable process. This should be an individual process and not a tool. We can see that process and the journey both child and therapist take together frequently becomes more important than the answers or "truths" found along the way. In short, the knowledge that a child may accumulate during their therapeutic journey is derived from dialogue and relationship.

CHAPTER TEN

Language

Working phenomenologically with children, the therapist is offered an insight into their world-view through their language. This may also present a greater possibility of disclosure, if they are able to take into account the assumptions that we all make towards another's understanding of a given word.

Each word a child uses may have a different meaning attached to it, a less rigid understanding than the way in which I may use or frequently encounter it. The world of each new child is like a foreign land with a unique culture different to my own, and yet grounded in historical context. The therapist's challenge, then, is to remain aware of the need to be mindful of different ways of understanding and coping with the world. Poetry, for example, as described earlier, is typically read in a different way to how a novel might be read. The reader expects the unexpected. The words, syntax, and grammar may be familiar, but we anticipate that each word will be layered with meaning beyond its everyday use. Similarly to the reading of poetry and verse, the language of children should not be analysed through an exploration of every possible interpretation or a search for a "deeper", more real, allegorical meaning. Instead, the therapist must be open to question and consider what first comes to mind and be alive to the narrative and disclosing message of the language.

The example of confidentiality

Perhaps the most common example of this in my work would be around the concept of "confidentiality". The work of most psychotherapists is traditionally thought of as completely confidential by its very nature, but in many settings rarely actually is. This is even more commonly the case when working with children, as others are legally responsible for them (as opposed to them being solely responsible for themselves), certainly in the eyes of the law, anyway.

A child of eight years of age is unlikely to have come across the concept of confidentiality, and the therapist will then have the benefit of being able to start at a point from which an original mutual understanding can then be constructed. It is not possible to say, however; that both parties enter the relationship with a completely clean slate, since, although the eight-year-old child may not be aware of the word "confidentiality", the therapist certainly is. Although words are given to us, that is to say, we are born into a world in which words already exist, when we then begin to use them we adopt them as our own. Each time a word is used our past encounters of that word provide us with some form of understanding for every time we have engaged with its meaning previously. Essentially, it represents a historical interpretation of all of these times. In other words, our understanding makes up the meaning of a word that we use at a specific time. This, in turn, is an assimilation of all the times that we have heard it previously. This meaning that we have partly constructed and partly adopted from our historical and social context will then also be affected by any new times we use that word.

If, for example, I describe a book as "blue", the blueness that I describe allows me to fit it into a categorization of my preceding experiences of a colour called "blue". The colour of the book is, however, a new experience, as I have never seen that specific book in that particular place at that time before. This use subsequently expands my possible understanding and future use of blue as a colour. In short, its spectrum has been increased. This is, of course, not to say each possibility is considered every time we hear a word, as clearly we would be overwhelmed by the world and paralysed by processes of trying to comprehend everything we encounter. This is simply an example of how our own personal history informs how we are, and the way in which we both see and understand the world.

In the case of the word "confidentiality", I may have a previous understanding of what the word has historically meant to me thus far in my life, but in its present use it has new qualities. When working with each child, the newness they bring to an understanding of a word like confidentiality would enable us both to be more focused on the present use of the word, and not allow our previous understanding to prejudice its new meaning but merely provide it with a historical context. This does not then have to become fixed; this would, I believe, not be very phenomenological. After both child and therapist have understood the word, although not necessarily in the same way, in each subsequent session it may evolve into something new. Every time the original (first session) understanding of confidentiality is stretched, distorted, or adjusted, it should be addressed and enter into a process of fluidity. The recognition of this change and the reflecting upon it is a core element of the therapeutic process as a whole. The core therapeutic value of trust will become inevitably compromised if I were, for example, to attend a meeting regarding the safeguarding of a child I may be working with therapeutically, without first discussing this with that child. Even children as young as four or five years of age can be made aware of what information will or will not be shared outside of the room, and they are equally able to enter into a negotiation around this. Any decisions made should, of course, primarily focus on keeping the child safe.

The mutuality of the understanding of new words is something that I would hope to negotiate between the child and myself. This can be difficult, and, if I am truthful, not always possible. Confidentiality is also a particularly difficult example, as it represents in its action something that is not entirely mutual. The usual psychotherapeutic relationship requires the therapist or counsellor to be confidential about the material of the children they work with, and the content of their sessions. However, conversely, the children themselves are able (and indeed may even be encouraged) to discuss their experiences of the sessions elsewhere.

Typically I would ask the child if they had encountered the word "confidential" before, to which the answer is usually "no". In my experience, children less than around twelve years of age rarely have, unless they have previous experience of therapeutic work. New words are often explained to young children by a comparison to other, higher frequency words, which it is thought they may already have some knowledge of. This is something I have done on occasion, but it is important that this is not performed in a lazy way and does not end simply at ". . . well, it's similar to a secret . . .". This merely allows the child to make his or her own conclusions about how similar or different these two words actually are. The word secret, for example, contains many differences from my understanding of confidentiality. Secrets typically carry consequences (particularly for the child) if they are broken in a considerably different way to confidentiality. A more thorough explanation should involve additional dialogue and an element of enquiry into the child's understanding and expectations. An active word like "confidentiality" acquires much of its meaning from the action itself; it is, after all, describing an action that is executed. Not only would I expect the relationship to remain confidential, in order to consistently illustrate some part of its meaning to the child, but also a hypothetical discussion of who I would not talk to could be appropriate.

Jordan

I saw Jordan in a room at his school that was used exclusively for counselling and was equipped with art materials, puppets, musical instruments, modelling clay, and other expressive resources that could be employed in psychotherapeutic work. Prior to the first session we had scheduled together, I took the opportunity to meet Jordan and introduce myself in the hope that he did not feel too worried about attending psychotherapy sessions and was able to grasp some idea of how our relationship would start. In this meeting, he had told me that there were stories he wished to tell. One of these stories was "Jack and the Bean Stalk". As soon as we walked into the room for our first session, he was very excited and energetic, appearing to show very little worry or anxiety about being in a new situation that was still unfamiliar. He quickly engaged me with a story he had asked if we could "make" using the puppets.

He was very directive, appearing to have a real sense of urgency to fit his stories and play, throughout his narrative into the time. This was the case for the first two sessions, leaving little opportunity for us to discuss boundaries and confidentiality in any detail beyond the limits of time, and the regularity of our meetings. This was important, as we had run out of time during the first session and Jordan had wished to continue his play the following week. On the third session, he began with wanting to play a ball game, which he had started at the end of the previous session. He also asked me to accompany him in a game, taking it in turns to make music using instruments. When it was his turn to make the music, he asked me how I thought he should play. I reflected back to him that these decisions were his to make, and there were no wrong choices in our play. I enquired at that point if we could talk further as the game and the music continued, to which he replied, "Yes, but not too loud, to put someone off."

I asked him if he knew the word confidentiality, to which he replied no, and enquired as to its meaning. We discussed ideas about secrets, and he told me a story in which a friend had asked him not to tell the teacher something. I tried to explain to him that he was able to discuss what happened in our sessions whenever he felt comfortable, but I would not repeat anything he told me unless I felt he might become physically hurt, in which case I might talk to his parents or a teacher in school (with whom he was familiar). He seemed to talk afterwards at some length about the difference of talking at home and at school, particularly around the notion of having to put his hand up when he wanted to talk at school, whereas he did not have to at home. I told him that he did not have to when he was here with me, and he could say whatever felt comfortable.

After we had finished playing the game, Jordan heard the squeaking of a door closing nearby. He told me it was scary. When I asked what he found scary about the sound, he replied that it could be a ghost. He continued by telling me that he did not like ghosts because they are scary and he did not really want to talk about it. "Can we not talk about ghosts?" I reminded him again this was his choice, but if he decided he did want to, I would not tell anyone.

Very soon into our discussions of contracting and confidentiality, Jordan had begun to negotiate with me around his concerns, testing to see how safe the space really could be for him. For Jordan, confidentiality was closely linked to choice; what he chose to say and what he chose to avoid. Although the rule of confidentiality was brought into the relationship by me as the therapist, it did not take away or reduce his autonomy and responsibility. In many ways, the language with which he was able to negotiate and build a mutual understanding of our contract set a context for the work ahead. The consistency and boundaries of the session were important elements of our practice, but just as central to our relationship was how he understood these terms, and what this revealed about his world.

Language can be seen essentially as a demonstration of our relatedness. When we name and describe the things we encounter through our day-to-day coping with the world, it is recognition of their absorption into our concern. Communication, in itself, is constitutive of our being, as we are always relating to the world. In turn this relatedness is language: whether we are explicitly talking or choose to distance ourselves from verbal communication there is always something being expressed.

The concept of language

Language is not an "object of thought". It is not a tangible "thing". It should not be introduced for discussion as an imaginary object comprising and assembled of real components. Language should *not* be considered, as it is so often described, as the "primary tool" of the psychotherapist. What takes place in a psychotherapeutic session with a child is a dialogue between speaker and listener that actively involves both parties. Although it is certainly true to suggest that both therapist and child must have some established understanding of the language they use, their dialogue is something co-created in the therapeutic engagement and not an object or tool brought to the room in the metaphorical pocket of the therapist.

In our very being, as humans, we are relational with other people and with the world. In the same way that we talk of our Being-in-the-world, we must talk of our language, not in the meaning that it somehow belongs to us, but in relation to our synthesis with language. "Language" is not an object used by psychotherapists, but really can be said to be inseparable from the very Being of the two people in "dialogue". "Words are connected with the primitive, the natural, expressions of the sensation and are used in its place" (Wittgenstein, 1979, p. 244).

Heaton suggests, in his brief comparison of the work of Wittgenstein and Freud, that language plays a momentous role in the very experience of emotions as well as the expression of them. He tells us that a child may experience the emotions of a feeling such as pain in a raw primitive way, such as crying and general discomfort. However, more complex emotional expressions become synonymous with the very words that describe them. A more complex and sophisticated emotional experience like "hope" can, thus, be said to be inseparable from the very expression of the word itself. With this idea in mind, it is possible to suggest that if a psychotherapist is able to increase the emotional vocabulary of the child they are working with, they will also be widening the possibilities for their emotional experiences. This is, I think, a controversial area, and it feels important to propose that in order for a new word to enter a child's vocabulary, it is not simply a matter of repeating to them a novel word that they are yet to experience. The word would have to be accompanied by a real experience that was not in any way inconsequential to the child.

Meaning and understanding

Meaning and understanding will inevitably be present in any exploration of language. However, to examine the relationship between language and objects with respect to meaning is similarly nonsensical. It is nonsense if I aim to find a point of connection or a process that exists. In other words, it is impossible to suggest that I can somehow step outside of language and see how it relates to me in a therapeutic context. However, considering how meaning comes to me, and how I am able to name objects does raise questions. Conversely, even the statement, "how I am able to name objects", is a presumption. It presumes there is something called I, and it is able to name what it classifies as objects. Both of these assumptions are questionable, and acknowledging this begins to ask how it is that we relate to the world and what role our meaning and language play.

The important notion to consider here is that these questions should be examined personally and individually, for any truths which may arise (or be formed) will ultimately speak of me and the temporality in which I exist. It is important to note that the relationships between language and "truth", or the bringing about of meaning, are not processes. As Wittgenstein tells us in *Philosophical Investigations*, "Meaning is not a process which accompanies a word. For no process could have the consequences of meaning" (2001, p. 186).

He goes on to make the comparison that a calculation is not an experiment, "for no experiment could have the peculiar consequences of a multiplication" (*ibid.*). It seems to me that the consequences of a calculation can be predicted in a way that experimentation does not allow for. Importantly, the process of the calculation is already determined, as it must obey a pre-existing set of mathematical rules. We cannot decide, for example, to multiply in a new and original way.

Understanding and meaning are revealed, then, not by the consequences of a process. What does seem to affect the way we understand, however, is the context in which meaning arises. This idea is well illustrated by Wittgenstein's example of the word "see". He discusses two uses of this word:

> The one: "What do you see there?—"I see this" (and then a description, a drawing, a copy). The other: "I see a likeness between these two faces"—let the man I tell this to be seeing the faces as clearly as I do myself.
>
> The importance of this is the difference of category between the two "objects" of sight. [*ibid.*, p. 165]

The difference he described is between being able to make an accurate likeness of two faces, and, second noticing a different aspect of the two faces that had not been previously seen. Although we can see the faces may not have changed, they are seen differently. The context, however, is different. If I draw a cube below, what would determine how we see it? Probably the text around it, as this provides a context for the cube: is it a box, or a brick, or a mathematical symbol? To a point, we may see the cube only in one way, but with a change we may see it another. What is this change?

Often, we qualify what we see now by referring to examples from our own past experiences. When we perceive something differently we might say, "now it's a . . .", but it is not the object that has changed only our perception. Wittgenstein again highlights another possible pitfall in this situation: "After all my visual impression isn't the drawing; it is this which I can't show to anyone. Of course it is not the drawing, but neither is it anything of the same category, which I carry within myself" (*ibid.*, p. 167).

What he is referring to here is "understanding" by means of reference to an "inner picture". This possibility falls down with a little scrutiny, but our personal experiences do appear to have some bearing on how we understand and how we relate to language. The similarity is that personal and individual experiences are constituents of our Being-in-the-world, which are disclosed through language.

Disclosure and context in language

As Wittgenstein's claim famously informs us, "the limits of our language are the limits of our world". The fact that I must first turn to language to explain the context of language already begins to reveal something about the system of examination itself. Put simply, it is impossible to try to extract a context of language from within our culture, or indeed any culture, as this already requires a stance. Implicit within culture is, for example, an agreement of what will be thought of as true or false. Importantly, it is in the language used that the agreement occurs. Again Wittgenstein provides clarification, "If language is to be a means of communication there must be agreement not only in definitions but also (queer as this may sound) in judgements". He goes on to propose that "It is one thing to describe methods of measurement, and another to obtain and state results of measurement. But what we call 'measuring' is partly determined by a certain constancy in results of measurement" (*ibid.*, p. 75).

Inherent in any measurement is some expectation of the type of result to be obtained. Really, when examining the context of language and searching for an answer, we are asking a question of ourselves (if we are willing to look). From "finding" an answer and proposing that something is true, it is possible to examine the underlying context. This questions the criteria that exist in our individual searching that makes the answer we find seem "true". In many circumstances, children are referred to a psychotherapist by a parent or professional concerned about their behaviour or the "wrong" choices they seem to be making. By accepting the referral, the therapist is often in danger of implicitly agreeing with certain judgements as true. There exist difficult situations where seemingly truthful and factual information may be presented on a referral form, or during interview, as helpful to the child for whom a service is requested. The context in this situation is all-important, and must, where possible, be looked at in great detail in order to uncover the judgements it may contain.

I am reminded here of a similar example of the disclosure of judgements in the writing of Szasz;

> . . . an applicant for life insurance may be asked if he has ever suffered from tuberculosis. Ostensibly the question requires a factual answer; actually its purpose is to uncover whether the applicant has had tuberculosis and, if he has, to alert the insurance company to this fact. Similarly, an applicant for a driver's license is asked his name, address, age—and whether he has ever been in a mental hospital; though these questions resemble one another in grammatical form, they differ in strategic import. [1965, p. 31]

The moral therapist working with children must be conscious of the implications that will be construed through accepting a referral for a child. The message conveyed in a referral can often be protectionist, whether this is in a reflective or prereflective manner. The therapist can find themselves in a position of agreeing: it is the pupil who is struggling to manage their emotions appropriately, not the teacher; it is the child who is uncontrollable not the parent; it is the "unruly" and outspoken child who needs greater boundaries, not more freedom or affection.

Heidegger and language

So it appears that language has its context, and one that can be said to be based on judgements of truth. However, the language we use is also much more than this in the context of relational Being-in-the-world and understanding. Heidegger rather poignantly describes language as "an act of violence that discloses being".

> Thrownness [Geworfenheit] and understanding [Verslenhen] mutually belong together in a correlation whose unity is determined through language. Here, language is to be understood as a [primordial] "saying" [Sage] in which beings as beings, that is, in view of their being, show themselves. [2001, p. 139]

As a further example, Heidegger's use of language in *Being and Time* could be described as an "existentiale" (a "given" aspect of our existence, from which we cannot escape, but only react). It could also be interpreted here as poetical "saying", as found in discourse. For the case of "language" as an "existentiale", it is necessary to consider the nature of "thrownness" as the understanding of being as being (a being as being is in view of itself) that belongs to the being exposed toward being as a whole. However, it is important to remember that this understanding of thrownness can only ever be a "thrown" understanding. This means that it is impossible to try to separate a meaningful definition of our thrownness from our own understanding. In this primordial sense, it is, thus, through language that beings, in view of their being, show themselves.

There are also circumstances in which something can be claimed as "being addressed", for language is also conversation. Conversation is relational and, as such, illustrative of being human as Being-with [*Mitsein*]. Heidegger uses the example of "stress" (2000, p. 139), which he claims has the basic character of "being claimed by something as being addressed". In this case, our language is not used to communicate something, but is the original manifestation of what is. We are also, however, as human beings, able to be addressed through being claimed by something, from our thrownness and "understanding". In this case, it is possible for us to be claimed as something to be addressed by beings because of the mutuality of our thrownness and understanding through language.

In short, our language makes possible a space from which an interpretation is possible.

These seemingly different ways of being aware of our language are perhaps not really as separate as may first appear. The possibility inherent in our thrownness and of our being, being shown itself, makes possible the possibility of being claimed as something to be addressed by a being. It is from this understanding that the "hermeneutic circle" enacts the parameters of our temporal being-in-the-world.

My understanding and subsequent use of the "hermeneutic circle" is that it represents the unavoidable connection between implicit pre-understanding and explicit understanding concerning the symbiotic relationship of the interpreter to that which is interpreted.

> The making-present which awaits and retains, interprets itself. And this in turn is possible only because, as something which in itself is ecstatically open, it has in each case been disclosed to itself already and can be Articulated in the kind of interpretation which is accompanied by understanding and discourse. [Heidegger, 2000, p. 460]

Heidegger here alludes to, I believe, the interrelation of interpretation, meaning, and understanding, which are all linked to context. He goes on to tell us that temporality is always interpreted in the first instance in the "there". "There", for him, becomes a temporal concept as well as a spatial one, and it is our familiarity with it that in each case drives our interpretations and their understanding.

Hermeneutic understanding

Heidegger uses the term "Hermeneutik" when referring to the interpretation of facticity, or, in other words, of our own *Dasein*. Here, he is suggesting that *Dasein* essentially interprets itself, and that this process of self-interpretation that *Dasein* makes is rarely done so authentically. In fact, I would say it would be quite hard to find a circumstance in which *Dasein* would self-interpret authentically, outside of perhaps an ontological state, such as anxiety, or, even more obviously, boredom.

There are, of course, other circles involved in the process of interpretation. It is only possible, for example, to obtain an idea of being from *Dasein*'s own understanding of being, and this, in turn, can only be arrived at through understanding *Dasein*. *Dasein*'s understanding of being is, hence, only understood when we already know what being is. Similarly to the examination of the search for an understanding of language, it is the methods that bear scrutiny, perhaps more than the measurements made. It is necessary to have some sort of structure *a priori* in order to have understanding and interpretation of *Dasein*. "To understand the distinction between existence and reality, we need to understand being in general as the 'horizon' of the distinction" (Inwood, 1999, p. 89).

Although the word "hermenia", from which "hermeneutic" is derived, is originally a Greek word meaning interpretation, Heidegger chooses also to examine it in relation to its very basic etymological components, connecting the word to Hermes, the messenger of the gods. In the book *On the Way to Language* (1959), he suggests the first meaning of hermeneutic is not to interpret, but the "bringing of tidings and a message". When Schleiermacher first standardized and systematized hermeneutics, he described them as "the doctrine of the art of understanding". I believe that attention to the word art is integral to be able to progress towards what hermeneutics refer to. It is important to be able to consider understanding as an art, and not a science. When tidings or a message are brought forth, it is not an objective process. The philosopher Jonathon Ree quoted from *Philosophical Fragments* in an essay he wrote entitled "Philosophical tales":

> When a man has his mouth so full of food that he is prevented from eating, and is like to starve in consequence, does giving him food consist in stuffing still more of it in his mouth, or does it consist in taking some of it away, so that he can begin to eat? [Ree, 1987, p. 118]

Ree quotes this allegory to illustrate how Kierkegaard ironically removes from his readers the heavy burden of objective knowledge. Hermeneutic understanding is not about depth or volume of objective knowledge, but of something brought forth. In this sense it no longer appears to concern *Dasein* and its existence, but the notion of being. Heidegger describes it as "the presence of the presencing" [*Anwesen des Anwesenden*]. *Anwesen* means "to be there, in, at or involved in something", but also, in a modern sense, is a "residence, or place of dwelling". Heidegger employs something of both meanings when he talks of "letting what is present come to meet us in the present". Man then essentially reveals itself by responding to the call of the presencing by revealing its message. This "presence of the presencing" is a twofold process, which is sustained by language. Thus, we can see again that, through our language, as I earlier posited in quoting Heidegger from Boss's record of the Zollikon Seminars, the relationship between "thrownness and understanding are . . . determined".

This idea can be explained further by Heidegger's example of art: "How can I know what art is except by studying pieces of art?" (Heidegger, 1959, pp. 149–150).

In the same way, it is possible to ask how we can know what language is except by studying it? Heidegger answers this question by suggesting that we learn about language through using it. We cannot learn about language by making it into an object and speaking about it; we must converse in language and make it our own. This supposition only functions, however, on the basis of interpretations that have already been decided in some way—how can we know that conversation is constituted by language unless we already know what language is?

This idea of an active engagement is reminiscent of Wittgenstein's philosophical plea, "Don't think, look!", which invites us to phenomenological engagement. It is possible to further our knowledge of the language we use through conversation, as long as this knowledge is not taken to be scientific knowing, but, rather, some form of preparation for our future understanding. It is fundamental to any existential analysis that we include ourselves in our engagement when working therapeutically with children, or with our relationship to language. Effectively, in therapy each child is learning more about the language we use through discourse. By engaging through language we are relating and disclosing something not only to the other, but to ourselves. It is discourse that also brings about greater awareness of the truths we construct and acknowledge. From this position, we are able to question them and really choose to disturb or change if necessary.

Steven

Steven attended a small church primary school, which served a diverse inner-city community. The school had referred him to me for weekly sessions, which took place nearby in a rather "medical" looking consulting room in a community health clinic.

In the session described below, I was moved by an intensity of experience, of being with Steven in a way that I had not felt before with him and rarely have since with any other clients. He arrived in a calm manner, brought to the session by his father, as he was each week. Steven's father, however, would often bring him late for sessions, or come ten minutes after the agreed time to collect him. When he saw me in the waiting area, he would frequently try to engage me in inappropriate conversations about Steven's behaviour at home, and the negative perspective from which he viewed their interactions. I had tried to address this need that his father felt to share information with me, but it still remained a recurring element of the work.

Having settled in the session, Steven asked if we could paint a picture of two men. He asked me to paint one, while he painted the other on the same piece of paper. They were shooting each other and being shot, simultaneously inflicting wounds, suffering pain, and continuing to hurt each other. His figure had a large broken heart, with lots of blood coming from it. He told me that actually it was a robot, and I enquired as to why it had wanted to shoot my figure so much. He replied by simply saying his was evil and mine was good. I suggested to him that robots are sometimes controlled by other people, but he informed me that his robot had killed its master, and it then started to send larger rockets and bullets towards my figure. The explosions depicted on my person grew ever greater in size, illustrated by Steven with blue paint. Soon, as the explosions continued to grow in size, my person became covered with the blue colour and, in turn, the entire piece of paper was blue.

He began to stroke the blue paint with his hands, which by now had become quite thick upon the paper. It was not long before the palms of both of his hands were covered in the blue paint. He then decided to coat both his hands completely in the blue paint, like a pair of closely fitted blue gloves. Through such primitive, tactile language he had created a tension. I initially felt on edge about the potential mess Steven could have made, and yet soon after I felt worried that the figure he created had been destroyed, turned into a part of him. It felt in that moment as if Steven was the robot, killing itself but compelled (even programmed) to continue and that I was being invited in to share its world. I was persuaded to join him, and soon my hands, too, were covered in paint.

At Steven's suggestion, we waited with our hands over the heater in the room for the paint to dry. While we waited, as we sat there together, I asked him what it might be like to have blue hands all of the time. I tried to encourage him to articulate this very new and novel encounter in order to offer him a choice of describing this different experience of a session. Until this point Steven (unlike his father) had always presented as a very quiet, boundaried, and contained young boy. He chose not to shout or verbally articulate his emotional experiences in this session; his language and communication through the painting seemed louder than it had ever been. I tried to encourage him to consider how he may experience himself with me in a new situation. What he needed, however, was not to articulate the words or gain insight through reflection, but to share the experience. To allow me a small window into his experience in that moment was enough. The therapeutic impact was immediate. The negativity he experienced from his outside life had led to him killing off so many possible aspects of who he may have wished to be, and yet he chose to colour himself, creating a new identity.

He commented on the texture of the paint on his hands and the cracks that appeared as he moved them, but he seemed reluctant still to really engage verbally. As we sat side by side, with our hands above the heater, I felt a strong communication between us that was about a shared experience—a dialogue. This was, for me, an experience that brought something to light; perhaps it originated from the initial discomfort of painting my hands and then allowing myself to enter into a playful, humbling language that reduced us both to the same shared situation. Whatever instigated this encounter, it was for me a strongly emotional sensation, and I felt that further verbal communication might have hindered the real dialogue that took place between us. At the end of the session, he washed his hands thoroughly and cleared away all the paints we had used. He even threw away the blue picture we had created together and a blue handprint he had made towards the end of the session. He left no trace of any painting at all. The silent intensity hung in the air. I found the quiet atmosphere of the session particularly intense and it appeared as though something different to previous sessions had been shared between us.

Within this brief extract from the time I was able to spend with Steven, it is possible to see the importance of the context of a shared language. He was acutely aware of the language and words his father chose to use with me when describing his negative expectations of Steven. His use of the image of a robot and my subsequent interpretation relied on a mutually "given" understanding and knowledge of what robots are, or how they could be perceived. Robots are either programmed to perform given functions or remotely controlled in the moment. The robot he drew was perpetrator and victim, both aspects of his own self-image, both aspects of his world-view. When it came to conversation and dialogue, however, Steven was able to push and stretch the boundaries of what was acceptable and comfortable for me, not through the words he chose, but by a shared experience upon which to reflect. The newness presented me, as therapist, with an opportunity to be thrown off guard, being less prepared and, consequently, perhaps more open to seeing his often quietly delivered words in a new way.

CHAPTER ELEVEN

Authenticity and anxiety

If an object is described as authentic, it is taken to be genuine and real. If buying a particular brand of watch from a shop, I might ask if it is an authentically made watch by the manufacturers it claims to be from. In order to test this, I may look at an example of one I know already to be genuine. If asked to look at a painting and provide an opinion as to whether it was painted by a particular artist, an expert would be expected to have studied other works by the same artist known to be authentic with a strong provenance. Is it an authentic Picasso, Rembrandt, or Cezanne? To test the painting's authenticity, as with the example of the watch, there must be a comparable and original template. In essence, this template is the "true" and authentic example against which comparisons are made. When we consider the authenticity of what it is to be human, however, it is not possible to find a definitive template. There may be people we admire or look up to, but there is no quintessential human being. There may be habits, behaviours, and actions about which we may feel more proud than others, but none of them is more authentically "us" than any other. In different places and under differing circumstances, every child will act and behave differently. At school, they may be described as very well behaved and well liked, but at home the same child may act in a frequently aggressive or violent manner. No one state or pattern of behaviour is more authentic than any other. They are simply two aspects of the same child.

Sartre

When considering the role of authenticity in psychotherapy from an existential position, it becomes important to hold in mind that we are always active in the world. We are always directional, making choices about our lives, and have the freedom to do so. As Sartre famously affirms in *Being and Nothingness* (1958), "Man does not exist first in order to be free subsequently . . .". There is no "real" self to strive for. There exists, however, in each of us, either child or adult, the potential to be called from our everydayness, being lost in inauthenticity, to be in a state of authenticity. In this state, we are explicitly being confronted by ourselves.

Heidegger

Both authenticity and inauthenticity are aspects of our existence (essential qualities of our existence, named by Heidegger as "existentiales"). The problem of taking Heidegger's *existentiales*, our characteristics of "Being-in-the-world", as the basis for a methodology, however, is the lure of hoping to induce some type of greater authenticity in the children who come for psychotherapy. Authenticity is not, as some therapeutic practice may indicate, something to strive for. This would occur out of a misunderstanding of Heidegger's use of the word authenticity, which was not intended to include judgement, or a representation of something superior. Not only do I feel that this could be inappropriate, but it is not something that can be consciously and deliberately induced, for, as Heidegger tells us, this comes only from the ontological state of anxiety.

Inauthenticity

In authenticity, we are "our own most possibilities", but this is not a "functional" state. As Heidegger tells us we are "everyday and for the most part, lost in the *they*", in other words, inauthentic. This is a state that allows us to function; it acts as a homeostasis for our Being-in-the-world. From this, we see that inauthenticity for Heidegger is not something upon which he makes a value judgement. It is not something to be avoided. Also, importantly for any psychotherapeutic methodology, we are not able to conceive of our entire Being-in-the-world through authenticity (it shows us possibility). For Heidegger, we know ourselves by our everyday actions, and relating to the world and ourselves through the ontic (our ordinary, day-to-day state of being). I am reminded of what has already been written above of Heidegger's understanding of our "knowing" the world, which is that

> Knowing the world . . .—or rather addressing oneself to the "world" and discussing it (logos)—thus functions as the primary mode of Being-in-the-world, even though Being-in-the-world does not as such get conceived. [2000, p. 85]

From this understanding, it is not necessary to engage within any psychotherapeutic process other than the commitment of addressing the child and therapist's interpretations of the world. It is not necessary to try to induce anxiety with the hope of a move towards authenticity.

Intersubjective relatedness

So, if a phenomenological psychotherapeutic method is to draw influence from Heideggerian philosophy, what should it involve, if not movement towards authenticity? As I have already intimated, the key to the construction of any phenomenological method must come from an individual. In the case of psychotherapy, the process of being with a child with the hope of change, or at the very least some greater personal awareness, lies in dialogue. Every time that we are with a child we enter into a relationship. For the hour spent with them, for the duration of the session, there exists an opportunity to illustrate, to each child the therapist works with their Being-in-the-world. As Spinelli explains,

> This position holds that, not only are we unique (as far as we know today) in our ability to be aware of our existence, but this awareness

> reveals an inseparable relationship between existence and the world. Our awareness is not solely subjective but rather, intersubjective. [1989, p. 108]

If this interpretation is accurate, then therapeutically we are not a constituent of a subject–object relationship, but are involved in an association that defines our very existence. The idea of intersubjectivity is one that lends itself to the psychological investigations and theories of people like Daniel Stern and John Bowlby (particularly in his later work, 1988) as it can then be interpreted into analysable data and material that can be clearly observed and recorded. Both parties become key to the relation of something new. However, this is not the quantifiable direction that I shall take here. Emphasis must be placed on an interpretational understanding of any idea of "self-concept" that may arise from phenomenological interaction.

In a Lacanian view of analysis (Lacan, 1994, pp. 136–138) we are told that the client is always wrong. He suggests that although clients may arrive in the process of psychotherapy claiming to engage with themselves and their issues, the issues they actually claim to be addressing they are really avoiding by the very fact that they come to therapy. They escape their relationships in life by turning to a new one with their psychotherapist. From this position, we could perhaps hope to act as a type of illustrative canvas from which a client may gain some awareness of how they interact and are perceived, and then take that knowledge forward to their outside relationships. This is perhaps an important aspect of any psychotherapeutic relationship. For work with children, it is frequently the parent or referring professional who seeks an answer from outside the direct predicament.

The child has the opportunity to experience, without any confusion of history and previous familiarity, a new relationship, from which their self-awareness may grow. I am not suggesting here that they will be able to find greater knowledge of something which tangibly exists and that they can call a "self", for I believe that this interactionist model provides information only about a "self" that existed just for that moment. The relationship must be real, however, and the therapist has to engage in this process, and not just think of his or her self, as a *tabula rasa*. The child who leaves the session after fifty minutes will not do so exactly the same as they went in.

What we can learn from this is the importance that should be placed on being aware of our interpretations of the child, and the understanding we may form of them. Philosophically, it is possible to say that interpretations we make act to conceptualize what we already understand. Interpretation, in turn, gives rise to meaning, which will work out the possibilities that are given in understanding.

Disclosure in anxiety

Although judgements of truth are disclosed in all our language and interpretations, it is perhaps easier for us to see this in the language of anxiety than in other contexts. This is due to the inherently disclosive nature of human anxiety: it is an experience in which we see ourselves. "Anxiety brings Dasein face-to-face with its Being—free for (propensio in . . .) the authenticity of its Being, and for this authenticity as a possibility which it always is" (Heidegger, 2000, p. 232)

Through anxiety we come face to face with ourselves and from this turn towards the world around us. This is indeed a process from which we may see ourselves in a new light, or in a new way from which our perception of the world will begin from a completely new point.

> He who is educated by dread is educated by possibility, and only the man who is educated by possibility is educated in accordance with his infinity. Possibility is therefore the heaviest of all categories . . . in possibility everything is possible, and he who truly was brought up by possibility has comprehended the dreadful as well as the smiling . . . and [he] has learned the profitable lesson that every dread which alarms [aengste] may the next instant become a fact, he will then interpret reality differently, he will extol reality, and even when it rests upon him heavily he will remember that after all it is far, far lighter than the possibility was. Only thus can possibility educate. [Kierkegaard, 1966, p. 140]

In *The Concept of Dread*, Kierkegaard, writing under the pseudonym of Vigilius Haufniensis, discussed the story and concept of original sin. To begin with, we are presented with Adam as unaware of the difference between good and evil; however, the "possibility of freedom" is awakened in him by the prohibition of the forbidden fruit. He powerfully conveys the message that sin and, essentially, choice are not created by something external, but exist within all of us. The "infinity" educating us, is, in fact, our own *individual* awareness of possibility. As Kierkegaard tells us in his own inimitable style, the links between possibility and anxiety are strong: in anxiety, we turn towards the world and see ourselves.

Anxiety is non-directional

It is important to note that the anxiety Heidegger describes is not a fear of something, or worry, but essentially everything and nothing. Fear is directional, and always linked to the world around us. I might, for example, be fearful or scared of travelling by bus, having previously had a bad experience on public transport. This is a fear *of*, or worry *about*, something. Anxiety is not pointed in one direction in the same way. Anxiety ironically directs us outward to the world as a whole, and, in doing so, highlights only ourselves. In therapy, it is the revealing of ourselves and our possibility which can rest heavily upon the shoulders of children. Commonly, people expect to feel greater levels of anxiety when they are at their busiest, and perhaps expect the same for children. In many situations, however, overwhelming activity can act as a distraction for the anxiety that comes to light when all else ceases. It is at this point that we are confronted with our choices and may become acutely aware of ourselves in a state of anxiety. Activity fulfils the role of white noise, filtering out difficult choices. Conversely, then, existential anxiety emerges from moments of individualism, and, in a metaphorical sense, moments of quiet.

As Vigilius describes it, anxiety is different from other concepts, such as fear, in that "it *is* nothing", and he asks, "What effect does nothing produce? It begets anxiety". This acts to highlight that we are, to such an extent, the possibilities that exist for us. He has also drawn our attention to the possibility of what actually is, from the possibility of what may be, ". . . dread [aengste] is the reality of freedom as possibility anterior to possibility" (1966, p. 38). Without distraction, a child may be confronted with themselves and an awareness of their choices, context, and circumstances. Anxiety is born out of freedom and choice. It is directed out to the world and a consequence of our being-in-the-world.

Anxiety is a precondition for the choices we have, and, while it by no means remains necessary for all, or, indeed, many of our choices, it holds within it the possibility of freedom. The possibility of freedom appears to offer profound choices as to how it is that we exist. For Kierkegaard, it was important to oppose the idea of sin with "faith", since, unlike virtue or good, it requires a specifically inward choice. The faith that Kierkegaard often writes of opens up the possibility for a "leap" into uncertainty. Anxiety is the state that precedes an awareness choice; it approaches it, but does not explain it. In this example, choosing relies on a leap of faith. The leap is qualitative, relying on truth and temporality. Again, as with language, there is disclosure in the truth we acknowledge.

Charlie

A community paediatrician concerned about high levels of anxiety referred Charlie. He was nine years of age when I first met him with his mother, and he had not been attending school for some time. When Charlie came for his first appointment, although keen to attend, he looked pale and gaunt and sat for the entire session wearing a thick padded coat and woollen gloves.

Both Charlie and his mother described how he had been affected by severe allergic reactions to many different foods, suffering anaphylactic shock after eating something containing traces of peanut as a five-year-old child. Despite this, however, he had remained an active boy throughout much of his childhood, even playing football for a youth team of a successful, professional club. They spoke to me about the assortment of medication Charlie had been prescribed, with little positive effect: his sleep patterns had become extremely disrupted and he often stayed awake for the entire night, later sleeping through the day. He had not been at school for a full day for about three months. Even though his mother encouraged him to eat as varied a diet as possible, it had become increasingly restricted over the past few months. Charlie suffered bouts of high anxiety with increasing frequency, and this greatly affected all members of his family. He initially agreed to attend a further assessment with his paediatrician, to ensure his physical development was sustained, and hoped to see a dietician who, it was thought, may be able to establish a dietary plan with which he felt more comfortable. His mother was open and honest about the impact of Charlie's overly dependent and demanding behaviour on her own wellbeing, and she had been attending her own counselling for some time. Charlie agreed to meet with me for weekly sessions at a hospital near to his home.

After our first few sessions, Charlie looked as if he was finding it a struggle to attend. He became less animated in his manner, he complained of further pain in his stomach, and he told me that he felt his anxious feelings would never be able to change.

We began our time together by exploring how he would recognize any changes if they were to happen and reflected on the achievements he had been able to make regardless of his physical difficulties and high levels of anxiety. None of this seemed to help. Charlie illustrated how challenging he found it to leave his bed when "things were bad", and the only way to bring himself out of this sensation was through lying down and trying to distract himself in some way. His preferred method was to watch films. When we discussed the school Charlie had previously attended, he conveyed to me a picture of great contentment, expressing how he was popular and academically bright. Within our sessions, despite Charlie's rather dour demeanour, he was very eloquent and presented his thoughts in a very logical and, on occasion, highly intellectual style.

Each week he attended without fail, and each week he reported to me how difficult he had found the time since we had last met. He gave details of his intentions to meet friends, but had been too anxious to leave the house, or had hoped each day to feel "well enough" to go to school, but had not. He added that his mother and brother both tried to remain optimistic about what he may achieve in the future, but he could not see an end to his current predicament. When we discussed his goals and aspirations, he projected an image of a successful person able to finish school and attend university, but he spoke without any real conviction. I felt as if the life was slowly draining out of Charlie and he was becoming more and more of an empty vessel.

Charlie drew an image of himself stuck behind a large brick wall over which he was adamant there was no way to pass. On our fourteenth session, Charlie arrived looking even more fragile than he usually did and revealed that it had been a genuine struggle to attend the session today but he had done so, having been encouraged by his mother. Charlie added that his difficulties were overwhelming, and there was nothing else in his life. It seemed disturbingly apparent that Charlie now strongly identified himself entirely within the role of an anxious child with complex allergies. There was almost nothing else he was able to see or experience. Charlie described how these "bad feelings" were like a filter on a computer, blocking out everything else in his life.

It had become conspicuous how he struggled to see any other choices for new ways he could be and how he could identify himself differently. At the end of the session, he started to draw a circle, which he informed me represented who he was. He divided it into two pieces. One was extremely large, covering almost the entire circle, and one was a tiny thin slither. Pointing at the large portion of the circle, Charlie said that this was his "bad feelings" and the remaining thin fragment was the rest of who he was.

Over the next few weeks we discussed many of Charlie's beliefs and opinions. We spoke about which friends from school he liked and those he disliked. We talked about how he felt our sessions were going and how he might like them to sometimes take a different or new direction. I was able to reflect back to him my perceptions of our relationship and disclose specific times when I felt more, or less, engaged in our dialogue. Through our relationship, I endeavoured to create an opportunity for him to develop a sense of his own identity. It had become important for Charlie to be able to open up his world-view and create opportunities and choices for himself. Without being able to acknowledge a world beyond illness and anxiety, it had become all consuming for him and was his sole focus. Fundamentally, he was interpreting himself and defining who he was as someone in a state of anxiety. Like the wall he had shown me in his drawing, or the metaphorical filter on his computer, this self-interpretation, albeit a chiefly negative one, acted as a block to Charlie exposing himself. Although this recent passage of his life was clearly a struggle, it also had the comfort of familiarity.

When confronted with only his own sense of being, feelings of anxiety became overwhelming, and to cope with this Charlie chose to hide and distract himself. He had been subjected to difficult physical experiences as a result of his "medical" symptoms, and these had progressed to governing huge parts of his life. Through therapy, Charlie was encouraged to confront the choices and responsibility he had previously chosen to suppress. He realized his experience of anxiety influenced so many of the choices he made, and, through opening up other ways of being, he would become able to see how he had allowed these feelings to rule his life. Charlie's physical repercussions, due to the extreme allergies with which he suffered, remained throughout our time working together and he did not return to school. He was, however, able to manage his emotional responses better and feel more in control of who and how he wanted to be. Towards the end of our work together, Charlie had arrived at a session excited to tell me about a recent occasion on which he had chosen to cook a meal for his entire family, which they had all eaten, including himself.

Conclusion

"My sentences are illuminating in the following way: to understand me you must recognize my sentences—once you have climbed out through them, on them, over them—as senseless. (You must, so to speak, throw away the ladder after you have climbed up on it.)

"You must climb out through my sentences; then you will see the world correctly.

"Of what we cannot speak we must be silent"

[Wittgenstein, 1998, p. 49]

By 1939, when Ludwig Wittgenstein had become a professor of philosophy and a fellow at Trinity College, Cambridge, it appears he had almost completely abandoned the notion of lecturing to students (Ayer, 1985, p. 11). Instead, he would hold classes in which he would present and discuss his ideas with a small audience of dedicated followers. Coupled with his reluctance to publish much of his work, it is possible to draw a parallel in his approach to that of Socrates, centuries before him. For both of them, greater understanding arrives only from wholehearted and personal engagement. It is simply not enough to read, or be taught, their ideas without a commitment and attention to our own individual experiences. Their philosophies, like the processes of existential psychotherapy, are not passive activities that can be reduced to a manual of techniques or clearly identifiable theories.

Throughout this book, I have endeavoured to offer an account of my own personal perspective of working therapeutically with children, and, in doing so, provoke debate. This book is not intended to act as a definitive handbook for the practice of existential psychotherapy, for this would be somewhat contradictory. Neither, however, is it my intention to remain ethereal or safe in the ideas I hope to propagate, for this, too, would hinder rather than initiate thorough consideration and future development in the practice of existential psychotherapy with children. The context and circumstances in which each child arrives and engages in a therapeutic process are unique and particular to that specific time. Each child arrives with their own challenges, responsibilities, and unique world-view. It is through the growth of dialogue and a new relationship, however, that the therapist may hope to develop an understanding of this world-view and encourage a new perspective or choice for each child with whom they work.

Increasingly, choice seems to pervade a way of life for children in contemporary western society, but in a highly superficial manner. Children are often encouraged to make choices about their behaviour, their schooling, their futures, and their careers. As a therapist visiting or working in schools, I hear teachers and parents encouraging a child to "make the right choice". Much of *this* choice, however, appears not to include any real awareness of responsibility and, therefore, differs greatly from an understanding of choice at an existential level.

Many children, such as Rhys (discussed in the preface), become categorized and identified through an ADHD diagnosis or by their challenging behaviour at an extremely early age. They are simply regarded as difficult to manage or pathologized, and not as struggling with the challenges of day-to-day life. This sends an important message to many children that not only are they unable to cope with their own emotions and feelings, but also that the adults around them, whom they hoped to rely upon, cannot tolerate aspects of them either.

If we consider that our own sense of identity and ontological understanding is drawn from our relationships, essentially our being-with-others, then it is important to consider the implications each child is given. Rhys was told, by implication from his diagnosis and subsequent medication, at just four and half years old, that he would be unable to handle and control his own behaviour. He was told by his pre-school nursery and later on his mainstream primary school, through only being allowed to attend for half-days or excluded because of his behaviour, that he was unlike the other children and unwelcome. His family experienced his behaviour as uncontrollable and effectively began to mourn for the child they had once wished for. Although Rhys found it extremely challenging to relate to the people around him, it is also these people who hold a responsibility for his own negative self-identity and who he had become. In short, the responsibility of choice is paramount for not only *his* being-in-the-world in order to develop a new and autonomous awareness, but also for those around him. Responsibility lies with the individual and the world.

For children, life often has an immediacy, which can so easily be forgotten in our daily adult life. The preoccupations of living frequently draw us towards a future encounter or distant goal. I have to work hard now, in order to save for my retirement; I cannot stop and enjoy my breakfast because I might be late for work; and so on. Children, too, are often fed these same messages, and acknowledged as maturing when they adhere to them, or criticized if they do not. If you do not study for your exam, you will not get into college; you must succeed at college if you want to go to university or have the right career; and so on. Working as an existential psychotherapist with children, however, can not only be a rewarding, creative, and engaging process, but also offer the gift of time. Regardless of the demands of schools, families, and society, children are concerned with their present circumstances; they are concerned with what is happening now, and, in effect, they have all the time in the world. For some children, who may have suffered terrible abuse or neglect, this gift may be taken away from them, and it is the role of the existential therapist, through a focus on, and attention to, the present relationship, to try to bring it back. This "gift" is, of course, a two-way process, as a focus on present relationships and truthful, lived experience presents a greater awareness of our choices. If we are able to be aware of where and who we are in a specific and particular time, then it is possible to see and understand life with a new clarity. This clarity is from being-with. It is a phenomenological understanding of ourselves as living human beings. The development of a child is a process of connecting to, and understanding, the world into which they have been thrown. To grow and evolve, they become aware of the language of life and the world of which they are a part. A newborn infant begins its life physically joined to its mother, and does not distinguish itself from others in the world. There is no subject and object, only the world now.

The importance of time is something I have not dwelt upon at length in this book, but is a crucial aspect of practising existential psychotherapy with children. To understand its influence more fully is perhaps a task for the future, but I hope this book will act as a catalyst for greater research and personal enquiry into many of the ideas that have been touched upon here. Although the existential questions and ideas of what it means "to be", and what it means "to be a child", have undoubtedly seeped into many aspects of child psychotherapy since its inception. Through beginning to uncover and name them explicitly, it is hoped that an opportunity can be presented to each therapist to question and challenge their own personal practice for the future.

REFERENCES

Ayer, A. J. (1985). *Wittgenstein*. London: Weidenfeld and Nicolson.

Baruch, D. (1966). Little mocking bird. In: C. Moustakas (Ed.), *Existential Child Therapy: The Child's Discovery of Himself* (pp. 30–45). New York: Basic Books.

Bateson, G., Jackson, D. D., Haley, J., & Weakland, J. (1956). Towards a theory of schizophrenia. *Behavioural Science, 1*: 251–264.

Bettelheim, B. (1983). *Freud and Man's Soul*. London: Fontane.

Bleuler, E. (1966). *Dementia Praecox Or The Group Of Schizophrenias*, J. Zinkin (Trans.). New York: International Universities Press.

Bowlby, J. (1988). *A Secure Base: Clinical Applications of Attachment Theory*. London: Routledge.

Bretall, R. (Ed.) (1973). *A Kierkegaard Anthology*. New Jersey: Princeton University Press.

Cannon, B. (1991). *Sartre and Psychoanalysis: An Existentialist Challenge to Clinical Metatheory*. Lawrence, KN: University Press of Kansas.

Cohn, H. (1997). *Existential Thought and Therapeutic Practice: An Introduction to Existential Psychotherapy*. London: Sage.

Cohn, H. (2002). *Heidegger and the Roots of Existential Therapy*. London: Continuum.

Cohn, H. (2005). Interpretation: explanation or understanding? In: E. Van Deurzen & C. Arnold-Baker (Eds.), *Existential Perspectives on Human Issues* (pp. 221–227). Basingstoke: Palgrave Macmillan.

Cooper, M. (2003). *Existential Therapies*. London: Sage.

Derrida, J. (1979). Living on border lines. In: H. Bloom (Ed.), *Deconstruction and Criticism*. New York: Seabury Press.

Descartes, R. (1966). *Meditations on First Philosophy*, J. Cottingham (Trans.). Cambridge: Cambridge University Press.

Descartes, R. (1993). *Discourse on Method and Meditations on First Philosophy* (3rd edn), D. A. Cress (Trans.). Indianapolis, IN: Hackett.

Esterson, A. (1972). *The Leaves of Spring: A Study in the Dialectics of Madness*. Harmondsworth: Penguin.

Freud, S. (1905d). *Three Essays on The Theory of Sexuality*. *S.E., 7*: 125–245. London: Hogarth.

Fromm, E. (1976). *The Sane Society*. London: Routledge & Kegan Paul.

Gadamer, H.-G. (2000). *Truth and Method*, J. Weinsheimer & D. G. Marshall (Trans.). New York: Continuum.

Gill, M. (1994). *Psychoanalysis in Transition*. London: Analytic Press.

Heaton, J. (1995). The Self, the divided self and the other. *Journal of the Society for Existential Analysis 6*(1): 80–81.

Heaton, J. (2000). *Wittgenstein and Psychoanalysis*. Cambridge: Icon.

Heaton, J. (2001). On what can be said. *Journal of the Society for Existential Analysis, 12*(1): 102–111.

Heaton, J. (2003). Personal communication in Conversation at Regents College, 28 May. Reprinted with permission.

Heidegger, M. (1959). *On the Way to Language*. New York: Harper and Row.

Heidegger, M. (1987). *Nietzsche III: The Will to Power as Knowledge and as Metaphysics* (p. 822), D. Krell (Ed.), J. Stamburgh (Trans.). New York: Harper and Row.

Heidegger, M. (2000). *Being and Time*, J. Macquarrie & E. S. Robinson (Trans.). Oxford: Blackwell.

Heidegger, M. (2001). *Zollikon Seminars: Protocols—Conversations—Letters*, M. Boss (Ed.), F. Mayr & R. Askay (Trans.). Evanston, IL: Northwestern University Press.

Inwood, M. (1999). *Heidegger*. Oxford: Oxford University Press.

Jacobs, M. (1992). *Sigmund Freud*. London: Sage (Key Figures in Counselling and Psychotherapy Series).

Kant, I. (1964). *Critique of Pure Reason*, N. Kemp Smith (Trans.). London: Palgrave Macmillan.

Kierkegaard, S. (1966). *The Concept of Dread*, W. Lowrie (Trans.). Princeton, NJ: Princeton University Press.
Kierkegaard, S. (1992a) [1843]. *Either/Or: A Fragment of Life*, A. Hannay (Trans.). Harmondsworth: Penguin.
Kierkegaard, S. (1992b) [1845a]. *Concluding Unscientific Postscript*, W. Lowrie & D. Swenson (Trans.). Princeton, NJ: Princeton University Press.
Klein, M. (1932). *Psychoanalysis of Children*. London: Hogarth Press.
Klein, M. (1988). *Love, Guilt and Reparation: And Other Works 1921–1945*. London: Virago Press.
Lacan, J. (1994). *The Four Fundamental Concepts of Psycho-analysis*, J.-A. Miller (Trans.). London: Vintage Press.
Laing, R. D. (1990). *The Divided Self*. Harmondsworth: Penguin.
Laing, R. D., & Esterson, A. (1970). *Sanity, Madness and the Family*. Harmondsworth: Penguin.
Merleau-Ponty, M. (1992) [1964]. *Eye and Mind: The Primacy of Perception*. Evanston, IL: Northwestern University Press.
Merleau-Ponty, M. (2002). *Phenomenology of Perception*. New York: Routledge.
Minton, S. (2000). A brief reflection on Kierkegaard's legacy to contemporary psychotherapy. *Journal of the Society for Existential Analysis, 11*(2): 81–90.
Nietzsche, F. (2004). *Why I am So Wise*, R.J. Hollingdale (Trans.). London: Penguin.
Palmer, R. (1969). *Hermeneutics: Interpretation Theory in Schleiermacher, Dilthey, Heidegger, and Gadamer*. Evanston, IL: Northwestern University Press.
Plath, S. (1989). In: T. Hughes (Ed.), *Sylvia Plath: Collected Poems*. London: Faber and Faber, reprinted with permission.
Plato (1957). *The Symposium*. Harmondsworth, Middlesex: Penguin.
Plato (1974). *The Republic*. London: Penguin.
Ree, J. (1987). *Philosophical Tales*. London: Routledge.
Shakespeare, W. (1980). *Hamlet*, T. J. B. Spencer (Ed.). Harmondsworth: Penguin.
Smith, D. (1999). *Approaching Psychoanalysis: An Introductory Course*. London: Karnac.
Spinelli, E. (1989). *The Interpreted World: An Introduction to Phenomenological Psychology*. London: Sage.
Spinelli, E. (2007). *Practising Existential Psychotherapy: The Relational World*. London: Sage.

Stadlen, A., & Stadlen, N. (2005). Families. In: E. Van Deurzen & C. Arnold-Baker (Eds.), *Existential Perspectives on Human Issues* (pp. 133–143). Basingstoke: Palgrave Macmillan.

Szasz, T. (1965). *Psychiatric Justice*. New York: Macmillan.

Szasz, T. (1973). *Ideology and Insanity: Essays on the Psychiatric Dehumanization of Man*. Harmondsworth: Penguin.

Tolstoy, L. (1982). *War and Peace*. Harmondsworth: Penguin.

Van Deurzen, E. (1990). What is existential analysis? *Journal of the Society for Existential Analysis, 1*: 7–17.

Winnicott, D. W. (1971). *Playing and Reality*. London: Tavistock.

Wittgenstein, L. (1979). *Notebooks 1914–1916*, G. E. M. Anscombe (Trans.) (2nd edn). Oxford: Blackwell.

Wittgenstein, L. (1980). *Remarks on the Philosophy of Psychology I*, G. Von Wright & H. Nyman (Eds.). London: Blackwell.

Wittgenstein, L. (1998). *Tractatus, 6.54, 7*, D. Kolak (Trans.). Mountain View, CA: Mayfield.

Wittgenstein, L. (2001). *Philosophical Investigations*, G. E. M. Anscombe (Trans.). Oxford: Blackwell.

Wolf, D. (2000). Everything you ever wanted to know about Heidegger (but were afraid to ask your therapist). *Journal of the Society for Existential Analysis, 11*(1): 54–62.

Wolf, D. (2002). Nietzsche's psychopathology. *Journal of the Society for Existential Analysis 13*(2): 297–308.

Yalom, I. (2008). *Staring at the Sun: Overcoming the Terror of Death*. Hoboken, NJ: Jossey-Bass.

INDEX

For Product Safety Concerns and Information please contact our EU representative GPSR@taylorandfrancis.com
Taylor & Francis Verlag GmbH, Kaufingerstraße 24, 80331 München, Germany

www.ingramcontent.com/pod-product-compliance
Ingram Content Group UK Ltd.
Pitfield, Milton Keynes, MK11 3LW, UK
UKHW022201190926
475702UK00003B/149
* 9 7 8 0 3 6 7 1 0 6 4 8 5 *